PRA̶
TEST
FOR CAR DRIVERS

PRACTICAL TEST

FOR CAR DRIVERS

Test your knowledge of all the
essential practical skills

by
Linda Hatswell BEd (Hons)

Revised by
Keith Bell
Approved Driving Instructor

The British School of Motoring
Fanum House
Basing View
Basingstoke
Hampshire RG21 4EA

ISBN: 978-0-7495-7176-4

Colour separation by Wellcom, London
Printed and bound by Leo Paper Products, China

A04728

Foreword

You want to pass the driving test and take advantage of the freedom and mobility that driving a car can give you. Do the following three things and you will achieve your objective – passing the test.

1. Learn and understand the **skills** of driving by taking lessons from a trained and fully qualified driving instructor.

2. Acquire the **knowledge** of the rules through your instructor and by studying *The Highway Code*. A key element of learning is to test and reinforce your knowledge. This book is specially designed for this purpose.

3. Take the right **attitude.** No one is a 'natural' or a 'perfect' driver. All drivers make mistakes. Be careful, courteous and considerate to all other road users.

The fact that you are using this book shows that you have the right attitude to learning to drive. So, remember, acquire the **skills,** the **knowledge** and the right **attitude** and you will pass the test!

CONTENTS

CONTENTS

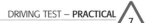

INTRODUCTION

by
An Approved Driving Instructor

GETTING A PROVISIONAL LICENCE

The driving licence is issued as a two-part document: a photo card and paper counterpart. So that you can legally begin learning to drive, at the appropriate date, you must have the correct licence documents.

Take time to read the instructions provided and take special care when completing all the necessary forms. Many licences cannot be issued for the required date because of errors or omissions on the application forms. You will have to provide a proof of identity such as a passport; make sure you have all the documents needed.

Make your application in good time; this can be as much as two months before it is required – for example, for a 17th birthday.

CHOOSING AN INSTRUCTOR

It is recommended that you learn with an Approved Driving Instructor (ADI). Only an ADI may legally charge for providing tuition.

Choose an instructor or driving school by asking friends or relatives whom they recommend. Price is important, so find out whether there are any discounts for blocks or courses of lessons paid in advance; if you decide to pay in advance, make sure the driving school is reputable. If lesson prices are very low,

ask yourself 'why?' Check how long the lesson will last. And don't forget to ask about the car you'll be learning to drive in. Is it modern and reliable? Is it insured? Has it dual controls?

A fully qualified ADI must display a green badge on the windscreen of the car while teaching you. Some trainee driving instructors display a pink badge. All Approved Driving Instructors are regularly inspected by the DSA.

THE HIGHWAY CODE

The Highway Code is essential reading for all drivers not just those learning to drive. It sets out all the rules for good driving, as well as the rules for other road users, such as pedestrians and motorcycle riders. When you have learnt the rules you will be will be able to answer most of the questions in the Theory Test and be ready to start learning the driving skills you will need to pass your Practical Test.

TOWARDS THE DRIVING TEST

The driving test is in two parts, the Theory Test and the Practical Test. Once you have a valid provisional licence you may take the Theory Test at any time, but you must pass it before you are allowed to apply for the Practical Test. There are a number of different driving books available, including the *Theory Test for Car Drivers* and *The Highway Code*.

It's important that you should not take your Theory Test too early in your course of practical lessons. This is because you need the experience of meeting real hazards while learning to drive, to help you pass the hazard perception element of the Theory Test.

TAKING THE THEORY TEST

You will have 57 minutes to complete the question part of the test, using a touch-screen. The test is a set of 50 questions drawn from a bank of almost a 1000, all of which have multiple-choice answers. In order to pass the test you must achieve a minimum of 43 correct answers within the given time.

The questions, complete with multiple-choice answers, are presented to you one at a time on a computer screen. You indicate your answer by touching the screen. You can go backwards and forwards through the questions and change your answers at any time. It is easy to use even if you have no prior computer experience.

Typically, five of the 50 questions in the Theory Test will take the form of a Case Study. All five questions will be based on a single driving scenario and appear one at a time.

The Case Study questions are taken from the DSA's databank of Theory Test Questions and also have multiple-choice answers.

The Government may change the pass mark from time to time. Your driving instructor will be able to tell you if there has been a change.

The test is available in a wide range of languages and can also be listened to through headphones for those with reading difficulties.

Hazard Perception

The aim of Hazard Perception is to find out how good you are at noticing developing hazards coming up on the road ahead. The test will also show how much you know about the risks to you as a driver, risks to your passengers and risks to other road users.

The test lasts about 20 minutes. First you will be given some instructions explaining how the test works; you'll also get a chance to practise with the computer and mouse before you start the test.

Next you will see 14 film or video clips of real street scenes with traffic. The scenes are shot from the point of view of a driver in a car and there are 15 scoreable hazards. As soon as you notice a hazard developing, click on the mouse control. You will have plenty of time to see the hazard – but the sooner you notice it, the more marks you will score. You need to concentrate on the test because unlike the questions section, you won't have an opportunity to go back to an earlier clip and change your response.

You currently have to score 44 out of 75 to pass. Check with your instructor or the Driving Standards Agency (DSA) before sitting your test.

At the end of the test you will be told your scores. You have to pass both hazard perception and the questions to pass your Theory Test, or you will have to take both parts again next time.

LEARNING DRIVING SKILLS

Driving is a skill that has to be learned; there is no such thing as a 'natural' driver. It's true that some people have a greater aptitude for learning driving skills but everyone will benefit from the tuition by a professional driving instructor (ADI).

The most efficient and cost-effective way to learn to drive is to accept that there is no short-cut approach. Agree with your instructor a planned course of tuition suited to your needs, take regular lessons, don't skip weeks and expect to pick up where you left off. Ensure the full official syllabus is covered and, as your skills develop, get as much practice as possible with a relative or friend – but make sure they are legally able to supervise your practice. They must be over 21 years of age and have held a full driving licence for at least three years.

TAKING THE PRACTICAL TEST

Once you have passed your Theory Test, and with your instructor's guidance, you can plan for a suitable test date. Having this goal to look forward to will help to maintain your progress and motivation.

Observer on the Test

Before you start the test, the Examiner will check all of your documents and ask you to sign the marking sheet to declare that the car is insured and that you have lived in the UK for at least 185 days in the last 12 months. He or she will ask if you would like your accompanying driver to accompany you on the test.

This will mean that your accompanying driver (usually your Driving Instructor) is allowed to sit in the back of the car and observe. The accompanying driver would not be able to take part in the test or help you but will be in a better position to discuss the test afterwards and give advice.

During the Practical Test

During the test you will be expected to drive for about 40 minutes in various road situations, some of which will be higher speed roads possibly up to the maximum 70mph. You will be asked to perform one out of the three reversing manoeuvres for which you have been trained, and you may or may not be asked to perform an emergency stop.

In order to pass the driving test, you must drive

- without committing any serious fault

  and
- without committing more than 15 driving errors of a less serious nature.

Independent Driving

Once you have passed your test you will be driving independently without the help of someone giving you directions. This skill is examined during your Practical. The examiner will show you a diagram and ask you to drive without junction-to-junction directions to assess if this skill has been learned. The Examiner will continue to assess your driving skills but will not be assessing your ability to remember a route, so you

can still ask the Examiner to confirm which direction you should be going in. Your driving instructor will help you to practise this skill and prepare you for both the test and the future.

Vehicle Safety Questions

You will also be asked to answer two vehicle safety check questions, one 'show me' and one 'tell me'. These questions are to make sure that you know how to check that your vehicle is safe to drive. One or both of the questions answered incorrectly will result in one driving fault being recorded.

Questions fall into three categories

- Identify
- Tell me how you would check
- Show me how you check

Although some checks may require you to identify where fluid levels would be checked, you will not be asked to touch a hot engine or physically check fluid levels. You may refer to vehicle information system (if fitted) when answering questions on fluid levels and tyre pressures.

All vehicles differ slightly so it is important that you get to know all the safety systems and engine layout in the vehicle in which you plan to take your practical test.

Examples of Safety Check Questions

? *Identify where you would check the engine oil and tell me how you would check the oil level.*

? *Identify where is the washer fluid reservoir how you would check the washer fluid level.*

? *Tell me how you would check that the brake lights are working on this car.*

? *Tell me how you would check that the tyres have sufficient tread depth and that their general condition is safe to use on the road.*

? *Show me how you check the horn is working (off road only).*

? *Show me how you check the handbrake for excessive wear.*

Your driving instructor will be trained to teach you about making sure your vehicle is safe for use.

If during learning to drive you have covered the full syllabus with your driving instructor *and* have taken the time to learn and understand the law regarding vehicle safety and maintenance (*The Highway Code*) you will be adequately equipped to do what is asked.

Those who pass the driving test first time are those who commit themselves to a planned course of tuition, have sufficient lessons and as much practice as possible, and then drive as they have been taught.

MORE INFORMATION

For more practical information on the Theory Test, Hazard Perception and the Practical Test visit www.direct.gov.uk/en/Motoring/.

Good defensive driving depends on adopting the right attitude from the start. These questions will test your knowledge of what is required before you even sit in the driver's seat.

1 What do you need before you can drive on a public road?

Answer _____

2 The best way to learn is to have regular planned tuition with an ADI (Approved Driving Instructor).

An ADI is someone who has taken and passed all three driving instructor's

e _ _ _ _ _ _ _ _ _ _ _ and is

on the official r_ _ _ _ _ _ _

Complete the sentence

3 Anyone supervising a learner must be at least _ _ years old and must

have held (and still hold) a full driving licence (motor car) for at least

t_ _ _ _ years

Complete the sentence

4 Your tuition vehicle must display L-plates. Where should they be placed?

Answer _____

HINTS ✔ & TIPS

A FULLY QUALIFIED ADI SHOULD DISPLAY A GREEN CERTIFICATE ON THE WINDSCREEN OF THEIR CAR. ASK TO SEE IT.

5 Young and inexperienced drivers are more vulnerable. Is this true or false?

Answer _____

6 Showing responsibility to yourself and others is the key to being a safe driver. Ask yourself, would you ...

		Yes	No
1	*Want to drive with someone who has been drinking?*	☐	☐
2	*Want to drive with someone who takes risks and puts other lives at risk?*	☐	☐
3	*Want to drive with someone who does not concentrate?*	☐	☐
4	*Want to drive with someone who drives too fast?*	☐	☐

7 Do you want to be a safe and responsible driver?

Tick the correct box

Yes   No
☐ ☐

8 You must pass a theory test before you can take the practical test. When would be the best time to sit this test?

Mark two answers

1 Before applying for a provisional licence ☐

2 Just before taking the practical test ☐

3 Some time during the early weeks of your driving lessons ☐

4 After full study of available training materials ☐

ANSWERS ON PAGE (117)

9 To use the controls safely you need to adopt a suitable driving position. There are a number of checks you should make.

Fill in the missing words

1 Check the h _ _ _ _ _ _ _ _ _ is on.

2 Check the d _ _ _ _ are shut.

3 Check your s _ _ _ is in the correct position.

4 Check the h _ _ _ r _ _ _ _ _ _ _ _ _ is adjusted to give maximum protection.

5 Check the driving m _ _ _ _ _ _ are adjusted to give maximum rear view.

6 Check your s _ _ _ b _ _ _ is securely fastened.

10 Here is a list of controls and a list of functions.

Match each function to its control by placing the appropriate letter in the box

THE FUNCTIONS	THE CONTROLS	
A To control the direction in which you want to travel	THE HANDBRAKE	☐
B To slow or stop the vehicle	THE DRIVING MIRRORS	☐
C To increase or decrease the engine's speed	THE GEAR LEVER	☐
D To give you a clear view behind	THE CLUTCH	☐
E To hold the vehicle still when it is stationary	THE STEERING WHEEL	☐
F To enable you to change gear	THE FOOT-BRAKE	☐
G To enable you to make or break contact between the engine and the wheels	THE ACCELERATOR	☐

Fill in the missing word

The accelerator can also be called the g _ _ pedal

ANSWERS ON PAGE 117

11 Which foot should you use for each of these controls (in cars with a manual gearbox)?

R = *Right foot* L = *Left foot*

The foot-brake ☐   The clutch ☐   The accelerator ☐

12 Are the following statements about steering true or false?   True False

1 I must keep both hands on the wheel at all times.   ☐ ☐

2 To keep good control I should feed the wheel through my hands.   ☐ ☐

3 I can place my hands at any position as long as I am comfortable.   ☐ ☐

4 When going round corners, it is best to cross my hands (hand over hand).   ☐ ☐

5 I should never take both hands off the wheel when the vehicle is moving.   ☐ ☐

6 To straighten up I should feed the wheel back through my hands.   ☐ ☐

13 Match each of the following controls to its function.

THE FUNCTIONS	THE CONTROLS	
A To enable you to see the road ahead and other road users to see you without causing dazzle	THE DIRECTION INDICATORS	☐
B To show other road users which way you intend to turn	DIPPED BEAM	☐
C To use only when visibility is 100metres/yards or less	MAIN BEAM	☐
D To enable you to see further, but not to be used when there is oncoming traffic	REAR FOG LAMP	☐
E To warn other road users of your presence	HORN	☐
F To warn other road users when you are temporarily obstructing traffic	HAZARD LIGHTS	☐

ANSWERS ON PAGE (117)

1 The following is a list of actions involved in moving off from rest.
Number the boxes 1 to 9 to show the correct sequence

The first box has been filled in to give you a start

[1] **A** Press the clutch down fully

[ ] **B** Check your mirrors

[ ] **C** Set the accelerator pedal

[ ] **D** Move the gear lever into 1st gear

[ ] **E** Decide whether you need to give a signal

[ ] **F** Let the clutch come to biting
point and hold it steady

[ ] **G** Check your blind spot

[ ] **H** If safe, release the handbrake and let the
clutch up a little more

[ ] **I** Press the accelerator pedal a little more
and let the clutch up fully

ANSWERS ON PAGE (117)

2 The following is a list of actions required for stopping normally. Number the boxes 1 to 9 to show the correct sequence.

The first box has been filled in to give you a start

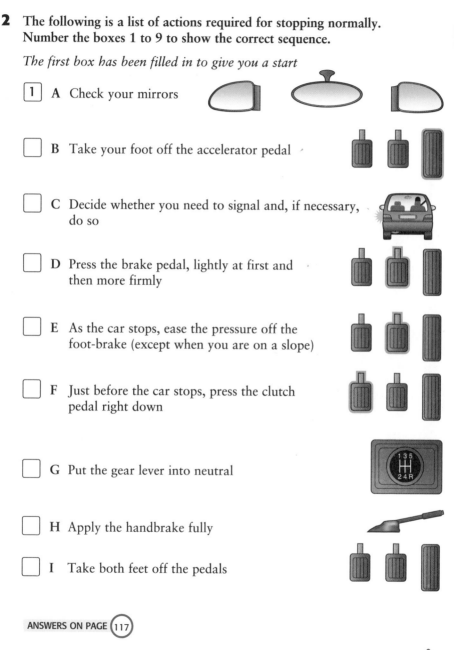

[1] **A** Check your mirrors

[ ] **B** Take your foot off the accelerator pedal

[ ] **C** Decide whether you need to signal and, if necessary, do so

[ ] **D** Press the brake pedal, lightly at first and then more firmly

[ ] **E** As the car stops, ease the pressure off the foot-brake (except when you are on a slope)

[ ] **F** Just before the car stops, press the clutch pedal right down

[ ] **G** Put the gear lever into neutral

[ ] **H** Apply the handbrake fully

[ ] **I** Take both feet off the pedals

ANSWERS ON PAGE (117)

SECTION 2

Gears enable you to select the power you need from the engine to perform a particular task.

3 Which gear gives you the most power?

Answer

4 If you were travelling at 60mph on a clear road, which gear would you most likely select?

5 When approaching and turning a corner, as shown in the diagram, which gear would you most likely use?

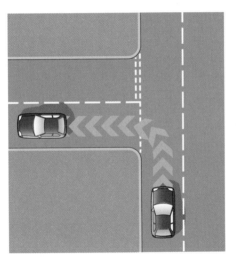

Answer

ANSWERS ON PAGE 117

6 You need to change gear to match your e_ _ _ _ _ speed to the speed at which your v_ _ _ _ _ _ is travelling. The s_ _ _ _ the engine is making will help you know w_ _ _ to change gear.

Complete the sentences

7 Number the boxes to show the correct sequence of actions required when changing up.

The first box has been filled in for you

| 1 | **A** Place your left hand on the gear lever

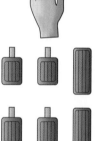

| | **B** Move the gear lever to the next highest position

| | **C** Press the clutch pedal down fully and ease off the accelerator pedal

| | **D** Let the clutch pedal come up fully and, at the same time, press the accelerator pedal

| | **E** Put your left hand back on the steering wheel

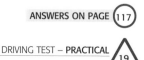

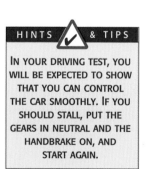

ANSWERS ON PAGE 117

8 Are the following statements about changing down true or false?

Tick the appropriate boxes True False

1 *I would stay in the highest gear as long as possible, even if my engine started to labour* ☐ ☐

2 *I would change down early so that the engine helps to slow the car down* ☐ ☐

3 *I would avoid using the foot-brake as much as possible* ☐ ☐

4 *I would usually slow the car down by using the foot-brake first. Then, when I am at the required speed, I would change down to the appropriate gear* ☐ ☐

5 *I would always change down through the gears so that I do not miss out any intermediate gears* ☐ ☐

9 When changing gear, I should look ...

1 Ahead ☐ *2 At the gear lever* ☐ *3 At my feet* ☐

Which is correct?

10 Do's and don'ts

Do Don't

1 *Force the gear lever if there is any resistance* ☐ ☐

2 *Rush the gear changes* ☐ ☐

3 *Match your speed with the correct gear* ☐ ☐

4 *Use the brakes, where necessary, to reduce speed before changing down* ☐ ☐

5 *Listen to the sound of the engine* ☐ ☐

6 *Take your eyes off the road when changing gear* ☐ ☐

7 *Hold the gear lever longer than necessary* ☐ ☐

8 *Coast with the clutch down or the gear lever in neutral* ☐ ☐

11 Which wheels turn when you turn the steering wheel?

   A *The front wheels*   *B* *The back wheels*

Answer

12 When you turn your steering wheel to the right, which way do your wheels turn?

   A *To the right*   *B* *To the left*

Answer

13 The steering lock is ...

   A *The locking mechanism that stops the steering wheel from moving when the ignition key is removed*

   B *The angle through which the wheels turn when the steering wheel is turned*

Answer

14 Which wheels follow the shorter pathway?

   A *The front wheels*

   B *The back wheels*

Answer

ANSWERS ON PAGE 118

SECTION 2

15 Which is the correct position for normal driving?

Put letter A, B or C in the box

Answer ☐

| A | B | C |

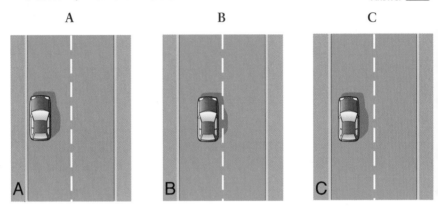

16 Which diagram shows the correct pathway when driving normally?

Put a letter A or B in the box

Answer ☐

| A | B |

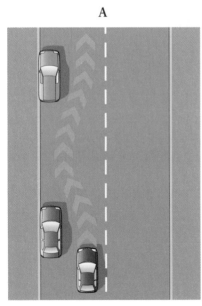

17 Pushing the clutch pedal down ...

   A Releases the engine from the wheels

   B Engages the engine with the wheels   **Answer** ☐

18 The point where the clutch plates meet is called the b__ __ __ __ __ point.

   Fill in the missing word

19 By controlling the amount of contact between the clutch plates, it is possible to control the speed of the car.

   Would you use this control ...

   Tick the appropriate boxes   Yes No

   1 When moving away from rest?   ☐ ☐

   2 When manoeuvring the car in reverse gear?   ☐ ☐

   3 When slowing down to turn a corner?   ☐ ☐

   4 In very slow moving traffic?   ☐ ☐

   5 To slow the car down?   ☐ ☐

HINTS & TIPS

REMEMBER: MSM STANDS FOR MIRROR, SIGNAL, MANOEUVRE. ALWAYS USE THIS ROUTINE WHEN MOVING OFF, TURNING OR OVERTAKING.

ANSWERS ON PAGE (118)

SECTION 3

1 A junction is a point where t __ __ o__ m__ __ __ r__ __ __ __ __ meet.

Complete the sentence

2 Here are five types of junction. Name them

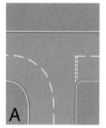

A

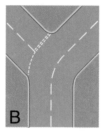

B

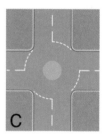

C

_____

_____

_____

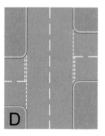

D

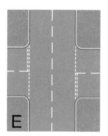

E

_____

_____

HINTS ✔ & TIPS

AT A STOP SIGN YOU
MUST STOP – BUT YOU
NEED ONLY APPLY THE
HANDBRAKE IF NECESSARY

3 Match these road signs to the junctions shown above.

Put letters A, B, C, D and E in the boxes

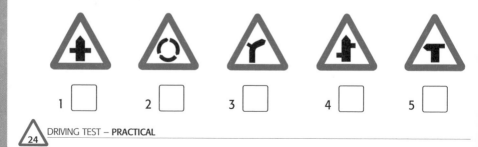

1 ☐   2 ☐   3 ☐   4 ☐   5 ☐

4 What do these signs mean?

1 Stop and give way

2 Slow down, look, and proceed if safe

3 Give way to traffic on the major road

Put a number in each box

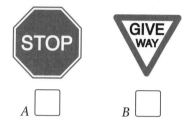

A ☐   B ☐

5 At every junction you should follow a safe routine.

Put the following into the correct order by numbering the boxes 1 to 5

☐ Signal   ☐ Speed   ☐ Position   ☐ Mirrors   ☐ Look

6 The diagram shows a car turning right into a minor road. The boxes are numbered to show the correct sequence of actions.

Complete the sentence

At point 5 you should look and

a _ _ _ _ _ the situation,

d _ _ _ _ _ _ to go or wait,

and a _ _ accordingly.

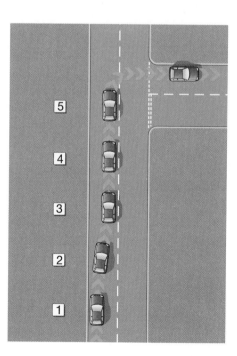

ANSWERS ON PAGE 118

7 Turning left into a minor road.

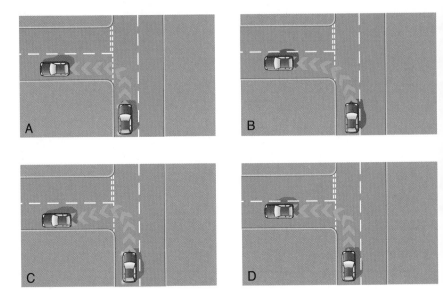

Which diagram shows the best path to follow when driving a motor car A, B, C or D?

Answer

8 You turn into a side road. Pedestrians are already crossing it.

Should you ...

Tick the appropriate box

☐ A Sound your horn   ☐ B Slow down and give way

☐ C Flash your lights   ☐ D Wave them across

ANSWERS ON PAGE (118)

9 Turning right into a minor road.

Which diagram shows the best path to follow: A, B, C or D? **Answer** ☐

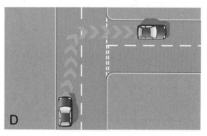

10 These are the golden rules for emerging from junctions.

Complete the sentences

1 Always use your m_ _ _ _ _ _ to check the speed and
  p _ _ _ _ _ _ _ _ of vehicles behind.

2 Always cancel your s_ _ _ _ _ .

3 Speed up to a s_ _ _ speed after joining the new road.

4 Keep a s_ _ _ d_ _ _ _ _ _ _ between you and the
  vehicle ahead.

5 Do not attempt to o_ _ _ _ _ _ _ until you can assess
  the new road.

ANSWERS ON PAGE 118

11 **All crossroads must be approached with caution.**

Match Actions 1, 2 and 3 listed below with these diagrams

ACTIONS

1 Approach with caution, look well ahead and be prepared to stop. Remember other drivers may assume they have priority.

2 Look well ahead, slow down and be prepared to give way to traffic on the major road.

3 Look well ahead and into the side roads for approaching vehicles. Remember other drivers may not give you priority.

Answer ☐   Answer ☐   Answer ☐

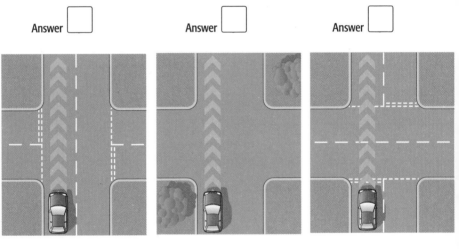

A   B   C

HINTS ✔ & TIPS

AT AN UNMARKED CROSSROADS, NO ONE HAS PRIORITY. BE EXTRA-CAUTIOUS AT THESE JUNCTIONS.

ANSWERS ON PAGE 118

12 Which of the following statements describes the correct procedure when approaching a roundabout?

Put letter A, B or C in the box

A The broken white line at a roundabout means I must stop and give way to traffic already on the roundabout.

B The broken white line at a roundabout means I must give priority to traffic already on the roundabout.

C The broken white line means I should give way to any traffic approaching from my immediate right.

Answer

ANSWERS ON PAGE  118

13 The following sentences give guidance on lane discipline on a roundabout.

Fill in the missing words

1 When turning left at a roundabout, I should stay in the _ _ _ _ hand lane and should stay in that lane throughout.

2 When going ahead at a roundabout, I should be in the _ _ _ _ hand land, and should stay in that lane throughout, unless conditions dictate otherwise.

3 When turning right at a roundabout, I should approach in the r_ _ _ _ hand lane, or approach as if turning right at a junction, and stay in that lane throughout.

14 The letters A, B and C in the diagram mark places where you should signal.

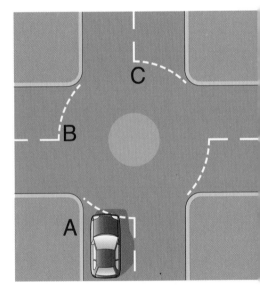

ANSWERS ON PAGE (118)

Complete the sentences

1 I would signal at A when turning _ _ _ _ _.

2 I would signal at B when g_ _ _ _ _ _ _ _ _ _ _.

3 I would signal at A and at C when turning _ _ _ _ _ _.

15 At a roundabout you should always use a safe routine.

Fill in the missing words

m_ _ _ _ _ _, s _ _ _ _ _, p_ _ _ _ _ _ _,

s_ _ _ _, l_ _ _.

16 What does this sign mean?

1 Roundabout

2 Mini-roundabout

3 Vehicles may pass either side.

Write 1, 2 or 3 in the box

Answer ☐

HINTS & TIPS

BE CAREFUL AT ROUNDABOUTS WHERE
DESTINATIONS ARE MARKED FOR EACH LANE.
MAKE SURE YOU ARE IN THE CORRECT LANE
FOR YOUR DESTINATION.

ANSWERS ON PAGE (119)

SECTION 4

1 It is safest to park off the road or in a car park whenever possible. If you have to park on the road, think ...

Fill in the missing words

1 Is it s_ _ _ ?

2 Is it c_ _ _ _ _ _ _ _ _ _ ?

3 Is it _ _ _ _ ?

ANSWERS ON PAGE 119

2 In this diagram four of the cars are parked illegally or without consideration of others.

Put the numbers of these cars in the boxes

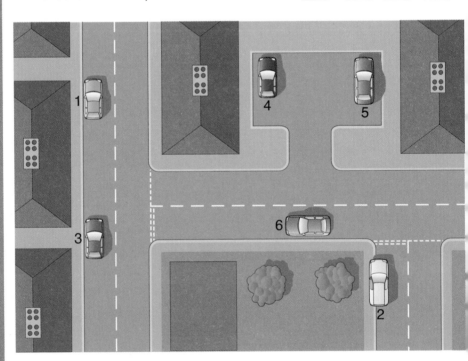

For reverse parallel parking manoeuvres, see pages 54–7.

3 Check how well you know the rules about where you may and may not park.

Are the following statements true or false?

True False

1 In a narrow street, I should park with two wheels up on the pavement to leave more room for other traffic. ☐ ☐

2 I am allowed to park in a 'Disabled' space if all other spaces are full. ☐ ☐

3 I should not park on the zig-zag lines near a zebra crossing. ☐ ☐

4 Red lines painted on the road mean 'No Stopping'. ☐ ☐

Tick the correct boxes

4 List three places not mentioned in Question 3 where you should *not* park.

1 _____

_____

2 _____

_____

3 _____

_____

HINTS ✔ & TIPS

USE YOUR *HIGHWAY CODE* TO FIND OUT MORE ABOUT PARKING REGULATIONS

ANSWERS ON PAGE 119

SECTION 5

1 The diagram shows a stationary vehicle on the left-hand side of the road.

Which should have priority, vehicle 1 or vehicle 2?

Answer

ANSWERS ON PAGE 119

2 This diagram shows a steep downward hill with an obstruction on the right-hand side of the road. Which vehicle should be given priority, vehicle 1 or vehicle 2?

Answer

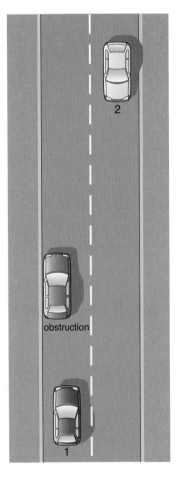

3 The diagram shows two vehicles, travelling in opposite directions, turning right at a crossroads.

Are these statements true or false? Tick the appropriate boxes

True False

1 The safest route is to pass each other offside to offside. ☐ ☐

2 If the approaching vehicle flashes its headlamps, I should turn as quickly as possible. ☐ ☐

3 I should always try to get eye-to-eye contact with the driver of the other vehicle to determine which course to take. ☐ ☐

SECTION 5

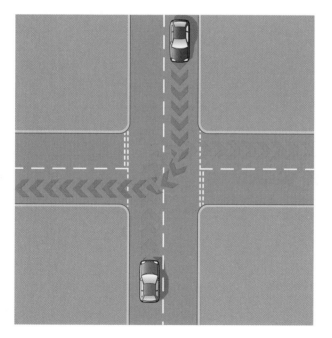

 ANSWERS ON PAGE 119

4 Which of the following factors, illustrated in the diagram, should be taken into consideration when turning right into a side road?

Tick the appropriate boxes

		Yes	No
1	The speed of the approaching vehicle (A)	☐	☐
2	The roadworks	☐	☐
3	The speed of vehicle B	☐	☐
4	The cyclist	☐	☐
5	Your speed (vehicle C)	☐	☐
6	The pedestrians	☐	☐
7	The car waiting to turn right (D)	☐	☐

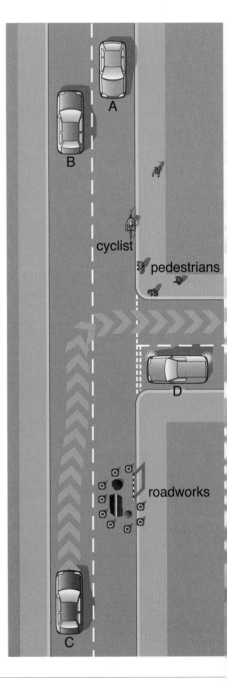

HINTS ✓ & TIPS

CYCLISTS ARE VULNERABLE ROAD USERS, SO YOU SHOULD TAKE SPECIAL CARE. PEDESTRIANS HAVE PRIORITY IF THEY HAVE ALREADY STEPPED INTO THE SIDE ROAD.

ANSWERS ON PAGE 119

1 Are the following statements true or false when stopping in an emergency?

Tick the correct boxes

	True	False
1 Stopping in an emergency increases the risk of skidding.	☐	☐
2 I should push the brake pedal down harder as I slow down.	☐	☐
3 It is important to react quickly.	☐	☐
4 I should always remember to look in my mirrors as I slow down.	☐	☐
5 I should signal left to tell other road users what I am doing.	☐	☐
6 I should keep both hands on the wheel.	☐	☐
7 I should always check my mirrors and look round before moving off.	☐	☐

2 Is the following statement true or false?

An emergency stop will be carried out on every driving test

Tick the correct box

	True	False
	☐	☐

HINTS ✔ & TIPS

ALWAYS KEEP A SAFE DISTANCE BETWEEN YOUR VEHICLE AND THE ONE IN FRONT, SO THAT YOU WOULD BE ABLE TO STOP SAFELY IN AN EMERGENCY

ANSWERS ON PAGE 119

SECTION 6

3 Cadence braking is a technique which can be used in very slippery conditions in an emergency.

Fill in the missing words

The technique requires you to p_ _ _ the brake pedal. The procedure to follow is:

1 Apply m_ _ _ _ _ _ pressure.

2 Release the brake pedal just as the wheels are about to l_ _ _.

3 Then q_ _ _ _ _ _ apply the brakes again. Apply and release the brakes until the vehicle has stopped. This technique should only be used in emergency situations.

4 Anti-lock braking systems (ABS)* work in a similar way to cadence braking.

Fill in the missing words

When braking in an emergency, ABS brakes allow you to s_ _ _ _ and b_ _ _ _ at the same time. You do not have to p_ _ _ the brakes as you would in cadence braking. When using ABS you keep the p_ _ _ _ _ _ _ applied.

Are these statements about ABS braking true or false?

Tick the correct boxes

1 Cars fitted with ABS braking cannot skid.

2 I do not need to leave as much room between me and the car in front if I have ABS brakes because I know I can stop in a shorter distance.

ABS is a registered trade mark of Bosch (Germany). ABS stands for Anti-Blockiersystem. The English translation is Anti-lock Braking System.

ANSWERS ON PAGE (119)

The distance taken for a car to reach stopping point divides into thinking distance and braking distance.

5 Could these factors affect thinking distance?

Tick the appropriate boxes

                                                 Yes No

1 The condition of your tyres   ☐ ☐

2 Feeling tired or unwell   ☐ ☐

3 Speed of reaction   ☐ ☐

4 Going downhill   ☐ ☐

6 Most drivers' reaction time is well over ...

Tick the appropriate box

½ second ☐

1 second ☐

5 seconds ☐

7 Stopping distance depends partly on the speed at which the car is travelling.

Complete the sentences

1 At 30mph your overall stopping distance will be __ __ metres or __ __ feet.

2 At 50mph your thinking distance will be __ __ metres or __ __ feet.

3 At 70mph your overall stopping distance will be __ __ metres or __ __ feet.

ANSWERS ON PAGE (119)

8   Stopping distance also varies according to road conditions.

Complete the sentences

In wet weather your vehicle will take l __ __ __ __ __ to stop. You

should therefore allow m __ __ __ time.

HINTS ✔ & TIPS

YOU NEED TO **DOUBLE** YOUR NORMAL STOPPING DISTANCE IN WET WEATHER – AND MULTIPLY BY AS MUCH AS **10** WHEN CONDITIONS ARE ICY.

9   Too many accidents are caused by drivers driving too close to the vehicle in front. A safe gap between you and the vehicle in front can be measured by noting a stationary object and counting in seconds the time that lapses between the vehicle in front passing that object and your own vehicle passing that object.

Complete the sentence

Only a fool b __ __ __ __ __ the t __ __ s __ __ __ __ __ rule.

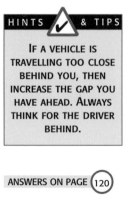

HINTS ✔ & TIPS

IF A VEHICLE IS TRAVELLING TOO CLOSE BEHIND YOU, THEN INCREASE THE GAP YOU HAVE AHEAD. ALWAYS THINK FOR THE DRIVER BEHIND.

ANSWERS ON PAGE (120)

1 **Are these statements about moving off at an angle true or false?**

Tick the correct boxes   True False

1 I should check my mirrors
   as I am pulling out.   ☐ ☐

2 I should check my mirrors
   and blindspot before
   I pull out.   ☐ ☐

3 I should move out as
   quickly as possible.   ☐ ☐

4 The amount of steering
   required will depend
   on how close I am to
   the vehicle in front.   ☐ ☐

5 I should look for
   oncoming traffic.   ☐ ☐

6 As long as I am
   signalling, people will
   know what I am doing.
   I will be able to pull
   out because somebody
   will let me in.   ☐ ☐

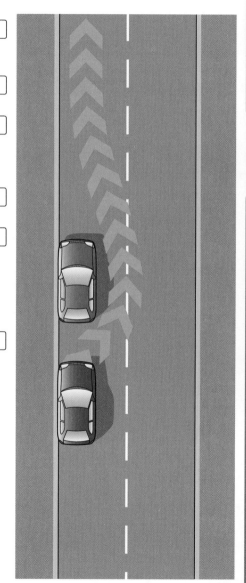

ANSWERS ON PAGE 120

SECTION 7

2 Are these statements about moving off uphill true or false?

Tick the correct boxes   True   False

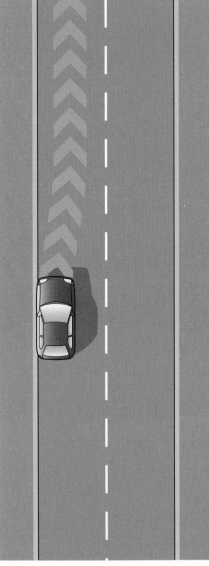

1 On an uphill gradient the car will tend to roll back. ☐ ☐

2 To stop the car rolling back I need to use more acceleration. ☐ ☐

3 I do not need to use the handbrake. ☐ ☐

4 The biting point may be slightly higher. ☐ ☐

5 I need to press the accelerator pedal further down than when moving off on the level. ☐ ☐

6 I need to allow more time to pull away. ☐ ☐

7 The main controls I use will be the clutch pedal, the accelerator pedal and the handbrake. ☐ ☐

ANSWERS ON PAGE 120

3 Are these statements about moving off downhill true or false?

Tick the correct boxes

True False

1 The car will tend to roll forwards. ☐ ☐

2 The main controls I use will be the handbrake, the clutch pedal and the accelerator pedal. ☐ ☐

3 The only gear I can move off in is 1st gear. ☐ ☐

4 I should release the handbrake while keeping the foot-brake applied. ☐ ☐

5 I should look round just before moving off. ☐ ☐

6 I must not have my foot on the foot-brake as I start to release the clutch. ☐ ☐

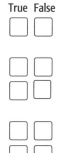

4   The following statements are about approaching a junction when going uphill or downhill. With which do you agree?

When going downhill ...

                                                        Yes   No

1   It is more difficult to slow down   ☐   ☐

2   Putting the clutch down will help
    slow the car down   ☐   ☐

3   The higher the gear, the greater
    the control   ☐   ☐

4   When changing gear you may need
    to use the foot-brake at the same
    time as the clutch   ☐   ☐

When going uphill ...

5   Early use of mirrors, signals,   Yes   No
    brakes, gears and steering will help
    to position the car correctly   ☐   ☐

6   You may need to use your
    handbrake more often   ☐   ☐

7   When you change gear, the car
    tends to slow down   ☐   ☐

ANSWERS ON PAGE ⟨120⟩

1 Before reversing there are three things to consider.

Fill in the missing words

1 Is it s_ _ _?

2 Is it c_ _ _ _ _ _ _ _ _?

3 Is it within the l_ _?

2 Are the following statements about reversing true or false?

Tick the appropriate boxes

                                                       True False

1 Other road users should see what I am doing and wait for me. ☐ ☐

2 I should wave pedestrians on, so that I can get on with the manoeuvre more quickly. ☐ ☐

3 I should avoid being too hesitant. ☐ ☐

4 I should avoid making other road users slow down or change course. ☐ ☐

3 How should you hold the steering wheel when reversing left?

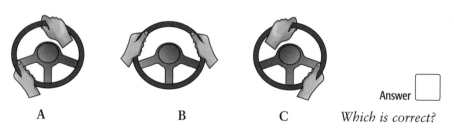

      A   B   C

Answer ☐

Which is correct?

ANSWERS ON PAGE 120

SECTION 8

4 These statements are all about reversing.

Tick those which you think are correct

	True	False
1 My car will respond differently in reverse gear.	☐	☐
2 My car will feel no different.	☐	☐
3 Steering is not affected. The car responds the same as when going forward.	☐	☐
4 The steering will feel different. I will have to wait for the steering to take effect.	☐	☐

5 Which way will the rear of the car go when it is reversed? Left or right?

Car A   Car B

Answer   *Answer*

_____   _____

ANSWERS ON PAGE 120

6 **It is important to move the vehicle slowly when reversing.**

Complete the sentence

Moving the vehicle slowly is safer because I have control and it allows

me to carry out good o__ __ __ __ __ __ __ __ __ __ __ checks.

7 **When reversing, good observation is vital. Where should you look?**

Tick the correct answer

1   At the kerb ☐   2   Ahead ☐

3   Where your car is going ☐   4   Out of the back window ☐

8 **Are these statements about reversing round a corner true or false?**

Tick the correct boxes

True False

1   If the corner is sharp, I need to be further away from
the kerb.   ☐ ☐

2   The distance from the kerb makes no difference.   ☐ ☐

3   I should try to stay reasonably close to the kerb all the
way round.   ☐ ☐

9 **Before reversing I should check ...**

Tick the correct box

1   Behind me ☐   2   Ahead and to the rear ☐

3   My door mirrors ☐   4   All round ☐

ANSWERS ON PAGE 120

10 Which position is the correct one in which to start steering?

A, B, C or D?   Answer ☐

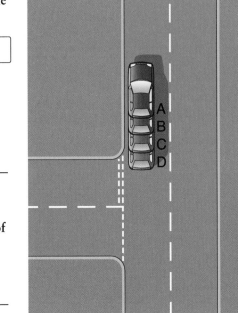

11 Which way should you steer?

Answer

_____

12 What will happen to the front of the car?

Answer

_____

13 Are these statements about steering when reversing round a corner true or false?

Tick the correct boxes

		True	False
1	The more gradual the corner, the less I have to steer.	☐	☐
2	I need to steer the same for every corner.	☐	☐
3	The sharper the corner, the more I have to steer.	☐	☐

ANSWERS ON PAGE (120)

14 As I enter the new road, I should continue to keep a look-out for

p_ _ _ _ _ _ _ _ _ _ and other r_ _ _ u_ _ _ _.

I should s_ _ _ if necessary.

Complete the sentences

ANSWERS ON PAGE 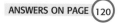 (120)

15 True or false? When reversing from a major road into a side road on the right, I have to move to the wrong side of the road.

Tick the correct box

True False

16 Which diagram shows the correct path to follow when moving to the right-hand side of the road? A or B?

Answer

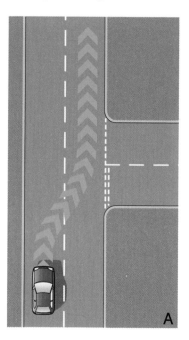

A

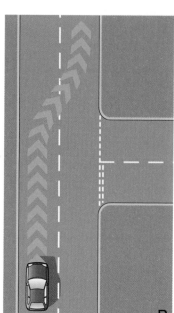

B

17 Which of the following correctly describes your sitting position for reversing to the right?

1 I will need to sit so that I can see over my right shoulder.

2 I will need to sit so that I can see over my right shoulder, ahead and to the left.

3 My position is the same as when reversing to the left.

Which statement is correct? 1, 2 or 3   Answer ☐

18 True or false? I may need to change my hand position on the wheel.

Tick the correct box

True False
☐ ☐

19 True or false? It is easier to judge my position from the kerb when reversing to the right than when reversing to the left.

Tick the correct box

True False
☐ ☐

20 Reversing to the right is more dangerous than reversing to the left because ...

1 I cannot see as well

2 I am on the wrong side of the road

3 I might get in the way of vehicles emerging from the side road

Which statement is correct – 1, 2 or 3?   Answer ☐

ANSWERS ON PAGE 121

21 How far down the side road would you reverse before moving over to the left-hand side?

Which diagram is correct? **A**   *or* **B?**   Answer ☐

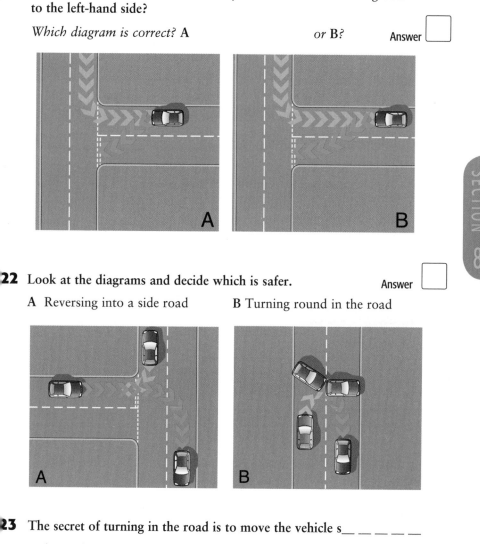

A

B

22 Look at the diagrams and decide which is safer.   Answer ☐

A Reversing into a side road   **B** Turning round in the road

A

B

23 The secret of turning in the road is to move the vehicle s__ __ __ __ __ and steer b__ __ __ __ __ __.

Complete the sentence

ANSWERS ON PAGE ⑫①

24 I must be able to complete the manoeuvre in three moves:

1 forward, 2 reverse, 3 forward.

True or false?

Tick the correct box

True   False
☐   ☐

25 Before manoeuvring what should you take into consideration?

Tick the correct boxes

1   The size of your engine ☐

2   The width of the road ☐

3   The road camber ☐

4   The steering circle of your vehicle ☐

5   Parking restrictions ☐

HINTS ✔ & TIPS

WHEN TAKING YOUR TEST, YOU WILL BE ASSESSED ON HOW WELL YOU CAN CONTROL THE CAR; SO DON'T RUSH YOUR MANOEUVRES.

26 Before moving forward, it is important to check a_ _ r_ _ _ _ for other road users.

Complete the sentence

ANSWERS ON PAGE 121

27 Turning in the road requires proper use of the steering wheel.

Answer the following questions

1 When going forwards, which way should you steer?

   Answer _____

2 Before you reach the kerb ahead, what should you do?

   Answer _____

3 When reversing, which way should you steer?

   Answer _____

4 Before you reach the kerb behind you, what should you do?

   Answer _____

5 As you move forward again, which way should you steer to straighten up?

   Answer _____

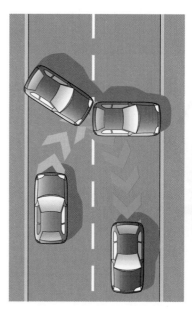

ANSWERS ON PAGE (121)

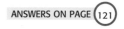

28 Reversing is a potentially dangerous manoeuvre. Good observation is essential.

Answer the following questions

1 If you are steering left when reversing, which shoulder should you look over?

Answer _____

2 As you begin to steer to the right, where should you look?

Answer _____

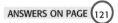

HINTS ✔ & TIPS

IN YOUR DRIVING TEST YOU MAY
BE ASKED TO REVERSE INTO
A PARKING BAY AT THE TEST
CENTRE, OR TO PARK BEHIND
ANOTHER CAR, USING REVERSE
GEAR. SO MAKE SURE YOU
PRACTISE THESE MANOEUVRES.

29 When parking between two cars ...

1 The car is more manoeuvrable when driving forwards

2 The car is more manoeuvrable when reversing

3 There is no difference between going into the space forwards or reversing into it

Which statement is correct? 1, 2 or 3?   Answer ☐

ANSWERS ON PAGE ⑫1

30 The diagram shows a car preparing to reverse into a parking space.
Which position is the correct one in which to start steering left?

Answer ☐

31 With practice you should be able to park in a gap ...

1 Your own car length

2 1½ times your own car length

3 2 times your own car length

4 2½ times your own car length

Answer ☐

ANSWERS ON PAGE 121

32 Use the diagram to help you answer the following questions.

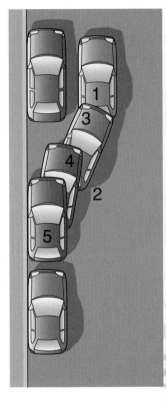

1   Which way would you steer?

Answer _____

2   At this point what would you try to line up with the offside (right-hand side) of your vehicle?

Answer _____

3   As you straighten up what do you have to be careful of?

Answer _____

4   What do you need to do to straighten up?

Answer _____

5   What would you need to do in order to position the vehicle parallel to the kerb?

Answer _____

33 True or false? During my driving test ...

Tick the correct boxes

	True	False
1 I will certainly be asked to perform this manoeuvre	☐	☐
2 I have to be able to park in a tight space between two cars	☐	☐
3 It may be that only the lead car is present	☐	☐

ANSWERS ON PAGE (121)

SECTION 8

34 When carrying out this manoeuvre, where is it important to look?

Answer _____

35 Look at the diagram and answer the following question.

Which bay should you use and why?

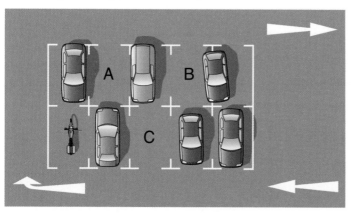

36 Why, wherever possible, should you choose to reverse into
a parking bay?

Answer _____

37 As well as being very aware of how c_ _ _ _ I am to the parked cars

on either side, I should also be alert for cars moving near me from all

d_ _ _ _ _ _ _ _ _ _, as well as the possibility of

p_ _ _ _ _ _ _ _ _ _ _ walking around my car.

Complete the sentence

ANSWERS ON PAGE (121)

1 Traffic lights have three lights, red, amber, and green, which change from one to the other in a set order. Number the boxes 1 to 5 to show the correct order. The first one has been filled in to give you a start.

Amber ☐ Red **1** Red and amber ☐ Red ☐ Green ☐

2 What do the colours mean?

Fill in the correct colour for each of the following

1 Go ahead if the way is clear. *Colour* _____

2 Stop and wait. *Colour* _____

3 Stop unless you have crossed the stop line or you are so close to it that stopping might cause an accident. *Colour* _____

4 Stop and wait at the stop line. *Colour* _____

3 Which of the following statements are true? Tick the appropriate boxes

On approach to traffic lights you should ...

1 Speed up to get through before they change ☐

2 Be ready to stop ☐

3 Look for pedestrians ☐

4 Sound your horn to urge pedestrians to cross quickly ☐

ANSWERS ON PAGE (121)

4 Some traffic lights have green filters. Do they mean ...

1 You can filter in the direction of the arrow only when the main light is showing green?

2 You can filter even when the main light is not showing green?

Answer ☐

5 The diagram shows the three lanes at a set of traffic lights.

Which lane would you use for ...

1 Going ahead Answer _____

2 Turning right Answer _____

3 Turning left Answer _____

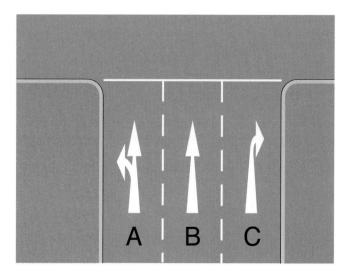

ANSWERS ON PAGE ⑫①

6 At some traffic lights and junctions you will see yellow criss-cross lines (box junctions). Can you ...

Tick the correct boxes

Yes No

1 Wait within them when going ahead if your exit is not clear? ☐ ☐

2 Wait within them when going right if your exit is not clear? ☐ ☐

3 Wait within them if there is oncoming traffic stopping you turning right but your exit is clear? ☐ ☐

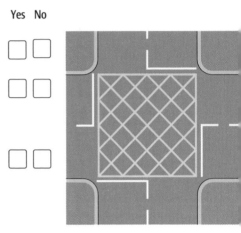

Pedestrians have certain rights of way at pedestrian crossings.

7 On approaching a zebra crossing, drivers will notice four features.

Name them

1 _____

2 _____

3 _____

4 _____

ANSWERS ON PAGE (121)

8   Are these statements about pedestrian crossings true or false?   True False

1   I cannot park or wait on the zig-zag lines on the approach
to a zebra crossing.   ☐ ☐

2   I cannot park or wait on the zig-zag lines on either side of
the crossing.   ☐ ☐

3   I can overtake on the zig-zag lines on the approach to a
crossing as long as the other vehicle is travelling slowly.   ☐ ☐

4   I must give way to a pedestrian once he/she has stepped on
to the crossing.   ☐ ☐

5   If, on approach to a crossing, I intend to slow down or stop,
I may use a slowing-down arm signal.   ☐ ☐

Tick the correct boxes

9   On approaching a pelican crossing, drivers will notice three key features.

Name them

1   _____

2   _____

3   _____

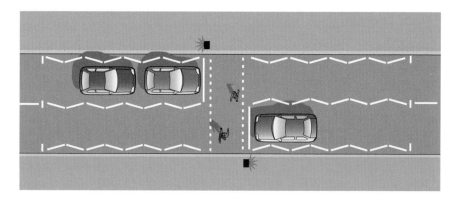

10 If you see a pedestrian at a zebra crossing or pelican crossing carrying a white stick, do you think ...

Tick the correct box

1 He/she has difficulty walking?

2 He/she is visually impaired?

11 The traffic lights at a pelican crossing have the same meaning as ordinary traffic lights, but they do not have a red and amber phase.

1 What do they show instead of the red and amber phase?

Answer _____

2 What does the light mean?

Answer _____

12 What sound is usually heard at a pelican crossing when the green man is shown to pedestrians?

Answer _____

13 Toucan and puffin crossings are similar to pelican crossings but with one main difference. Name it.

Answer _____

ANSWERS ON PAGE 122

14 As well as pedestrians, what other type of road users should you watch for at a toucan crossing?

Answer _____

A level crossing is where the road crosses at a railway line. It is potentially dangerous and should be approached with caution.

15 Match each traffic sign below with its correct meaning.

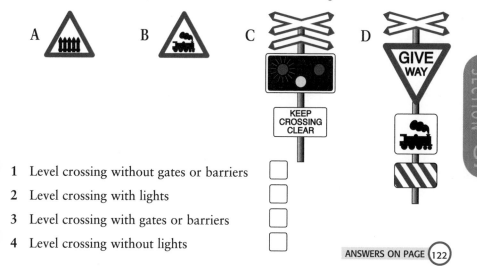

A   B   C   D

1   Level crossing without gates or barriers ☐

2   Level crossing with lights ☐

3   Level crossing with gates or barriers ☐

4   Level crossing without lights ☐

ANSWERS ON PAGE 122

16 If you break down on a level crossing, should you ...

1   Tell your passengers to wait in the vehicle while you go to get help? ☐

2   Get everybody out and clear of the crossing? ☐

3   Telephone the police? ☐

4   Telephone the signal operator? ☐

5   If there is still time, push your car clear of the crossing? ☐

Tick the appropriate boxes

One-way systems are where all traffic flows in the same direction.

1 Which of these signs means one-way traffic?

A

B

2 Are these statements about one-way systems true or false?

	True	False
1 In one-way streets traffic can pass me on both sides.	☐	☐
2 Roundabouts are one-way systems.	☐	☐
3 For normal driving I should stay on the left.	☐	☐
4 I should look out for road markings and get in lane early.	☐	☐

Tick the correct boxes

As a rule, the more paint on the road, the more important the message.

3 Road markings are divided into three categories.

Fill in the missing words

1 Those which give i__ __ __ __ __ __ __ __ __ __ __.

2 Those which give w__ __ __ __ __ __.

3 Those which give o__ __ __ __ __.

ANSWERS ON PAGE 122

SECTION 10

4 There are two main advantages which road markings have over other traffic signs. Name them

1 _____

2 _____

5 What do these lines across the road mean?

1 Stop and give way

2 Give priority to traffic coming from the immediate right.

3 Give way to traffic coming from the right.

Answer ☐

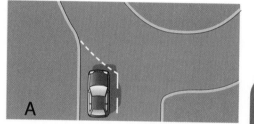

A

1 Give way to traffic on the major road.

2 Stop at the line and give way to traffic on the major road.

Answer ☐

B

SECTION 10

ANSWERS ON PAGE 122

6 Where you see double solid white lines painted along the centre of the road, what does this mean?

1 I must not park or wait on the carriageway. ☐

2 I can park between 7pm and 7am. ☐

3 I must not overtake. ☐

4 I must not cross the white line except to turn right or in circumstances beyond my control. ☐

More than one answer may be correct.
Tick any boxes you think are appropriate.

7 What is the purpose of these hatched markings (chevrons)?

Answer _____

_____

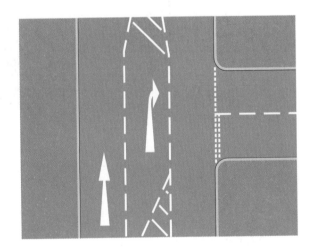

ANSWERS ON PAGE 12

8 What does it mean if the chevrons are edged with a solid white line?

Answer _____

_____

_____

The shape and colour of a sign will help you understand what it means.

9 Look at the sign shapes below and say whether each gives an order, a warning or information.

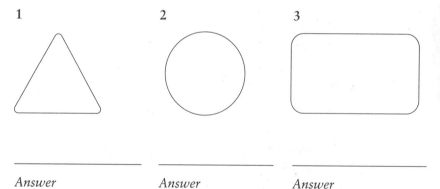

1

2

3

Answer   *Answer*   *Answer*

10 1 A circular sign with a blue background tells you what

you m__ __ __ do.

2 A circular sign with a red border tells you what you

m__ __ __ n__ __ do.

Complete the sentences

ANSWERS ON PAGE (122)

SECTION

10

11 What do these signs mean?

1 *Answer*

_____

_____

_____

2 *Answer*

_____

_____

_____

12 Some junctions have a stop sign, others have a give way sign.

Complete the sentence

A stop sign is usually placed at a junction where

v_ _ _ _ _ _ _ _ _ is l_ _ _ _ _ _.

ANSWERS ON PAGE 122

13 Information signs are colour-coded.

Match each of the following signs to its colouring.

A White letters on a brown background

B Black letters on a white background

C Black letters on a white background with a blue border

D White letters on a blue background with a white border

E White letters on a green background, yellow route numbers with a white border

MOTORWAY SIGNS ☐

PRIMARY ROUTES ☐

OTHER ROUTES ☐

LOCAL PLACES ☐

TOURIST SIGNS ☐

1 Good observation is vital in today's busy traffic.

Complete the sentence

When using my mirrors I should try to make a mental note of the

s_ _ _ _, b_ _ _ _ _ _ _ _ and i_ _ _ _ _ _ _ _ _ of

the driver behind.

2 Driving in built-up areas is potentially dangerous.

ANSWERS ON PAGE (123)

Look at this diagram

1   What action should the
    driver of car A take?
    List four options

    A _____

    B _____

    C _____

    D _____

2   What action should the
    driver of car B take?
    List four options

    A _____

    B _____

    C _____

    D _____

pedestrians

P

cyclist

B

SECTION 11

3 Motor cyclists are often less visible than other road users.

Complete this well-known phrase

Think once, think twice, think b__ __ __.

 ANSWERS ON PAGE 123

4 When you observe traffic following too close behind you, would you

Tick the correct box

1 Speed up to create a bigger gap? ☐

2 Touch your brake lights to warn the
following driver? ☐

3 Keep to a safe speed, and keep checking
the behaviour and intentions of the
following driver? ☐

> HINTS ✔ & TIPS
>
> **OBSERVATION MEANS
> LOOKING ALL AROUND
> AND SEEING ANYTHING
> THAT MATTERS. DON'T
> STARE AT JUST ONE
> THING – KEEP YOUR
> EYES MOVING.**

5 Some hazards are potential, others are actual and there all the time,
such as a bend in the road.

A Name five more actual hazards

1 _____

2 _____

3 _____

4 _____

5 _____

B Name five potential hazards, such as a dog off its lead

1 _____

2 _____

3 _____

4 _____

5 _____

SECTION 11

6 Modern driving requires full concentration.

Are the following statements true or false?   True False

1 Carrying a mobile phone can reduce the stress of a
long journey.   ☐ ☐

2 I must not use a hand-held phone while driving.   ☐ ☐

3 Conversation on a hands-free phone can still distract
my attention.   ☐ ☐

4 I should pull up in a safe place to make or receive calls. ☐ ☐

7 When driving, all the following actions have something in common.

Reading a map   *Answer* _____

Eating   _____

Changing a cassette   _____

Listening to loud music   _____

What is it?

ANSWERS ON PAGE (123)

SECTION 11

One of the features of driving on the open road is taking bends properly.

8 As a rule you should be travelling at the correct s_ _ _ _, using the
correct g_ _ _, and be in the correct p_ _ _ _ _ _ _.

9 Should you brake ...

1 Before you enter the bend?   ☐

2 As you enter the bend?   ☐

3 While negotiating the bend?   ☐

Tick the appropriate box

10 Which way does force push a car on a bend?

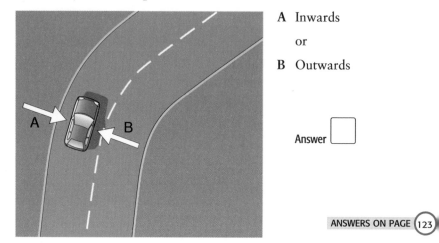

A Inwards

or

B Outwards

Answer

ANSWERS ON PAGE 123

11 What happens to the weight of the car when you use the brakes?

A It is thrown forwards   B It remains even   C It is thrown back

Answer

12 When you approach a bend, what position should you be in?

A   On a right-hand bend

I should keep to the

_____

B   On a left-hand bend

I should keep to the

_____

Complete the sentences

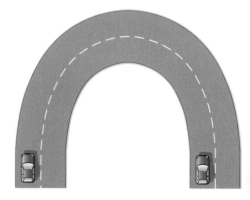

Overtaking is a potentially dangerous manoeuvre.

13 Before overtaking, consider whether it is really n_ _ _ _ _ _ _ _.

Fill in the missing word

Always use the safety routine when overtaking.

Put these actions into their correct sequence by putting numbers 1 to 7, as seen in the diagram, in the boxes

☐ Signal   ☐ Mirrors   ☐ Look   ☐ Position

☐ Mirrors   ☐ Speed   ☐ Manoeuvre

14 What is the minimum amount of clearance you should give a cyclist or motor cyclist?

Answer _____

 ANSWERS ON PAGE (123)

15 There are four situations in which you may, with caution, overtake on the left-hand side of the car in front.

Name them

1 _____

2 _____

3 _____

4 _____

16 List four places where it would be dangerous to overtake.

1 _____

2 _____

3 _____

4 _____

17 Dual carriageways can appear similar to motorways, but there are important differences.

Which of the following statements apply to dual carriageways?

Tick the relevant boxes

1 Reflective studs are not used. ☐

2 Cyclists are allowed. ☐

3 The speed limit is always 60mph. ☐

4 You cannot turn right to enter or leave a dual carriageway. ☐

5 Milk floats and slow moving farm vehicles are prohibited. ☐

ANSWERS ON PAGE (123)

18 When turning right from a minor road on to a dual carriageway, where would you wait ...

A When there is a wide central reserve?

Answer _____

B When the central reserve is too narrow for your car?

Answer _____

19 When travelling at 70mph on a dual carriageway, which lane would you use?

Answer _____

20 What do these signs mean?

A

Answer

_____

B

Answer

_____

C

Answer

_____

ANSWERS ON PAGE (124)

SECTION 11

21 Which of the signs in Question 20 (see previous page) would you expect to see on a dual carriageway?

Answer _____

22 Why is it important to plan your movements especially early when leaving a dual carriageway to the right?

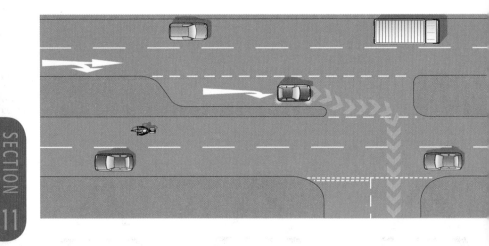

Answer _____

_____

_____

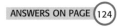ANSWERS ON PAGE (124)

1 Cars fitted with automatic transmission select the gear depending on the road speed and the load on the engine. They therefore have no c_ _ _ _ _ pedal.

Fill in the missing word

2 The advantages of an automatic car are ...

1 _____

2 _____

3 The gear selector has the same function as a manual selector, but what function do each of the following have?

P	
R	
N	
D	
3	
2	
1	

Park _____

Reverse _____

Neutral _____

Drive _____

3rd _____

2nd _____

1st _____

ANSWERS ON PAGE 124

SECTION 12

4 Automatic cars have a device called a kickdown. Is its function ...

1   To select a higher gear?

2   To select a lower gear manually?

3   To provide quick acceleration when needed?

Tick the correct box

5 When driving an automatic car, would you select a lower gear ...   Yes   No

1   To control speed when going down a steep hill?

2   To slow the car down in normal driving?

3   When going uphill?

4   To overtake, in certain circumstances?

5   When manoeuvring?

6   Before stopping?

Tick the correct boxes

6 An automatic car has two foot pedals, the foot-brake and the accelerator.

For normal driving, which foot would you use ...

1   For the brake?   *Answer* _____

2   For the accelerator?   *Answer* _____

ANSWERS ON PAGE (124)

SECTION 12

7 When you are driving an automatic car, using one foot to control both pedals is preferable to using both the left and the right foot. Why?

Answer _____

_____

_____

8 Some cars with automatic transmission have a tendency to 'creep'.

Which gears allow the car to creep?

Answer _____

_____

_____

9 When driving an automatic car, would you use the handbrake ...

1 More than in a manual car? ☐

2 The same? ☐

3 Less? ☐

Tick the correct box

HINTS ✔ & TIPS

REMEMBER – IF YOU HAVEN'T GOT YOUR FOOT ON THE BRAKE WHEN YOU SELECT DRIVE IN AN AUTOMATIC CAR, THE VEHICLE MAY BEGIN TO MOVE FORWARD

ANSWERS ON PAGE (124)

SECTION 12

10 In which position should the gear selector be when you are starting the engine?

Answer _____ *or* _____

11 As you approach a bend, an automatic car will sometimes change up because there is less pressure on the accelerator.

What should you do to prevent this happening?

1 Slow down before the bend and accelerate gently as you turn. ☐

2 Brake as you go round the bend. ☐

3 Brake and accelerate at the same time. ☐

ANSWERS ON PAGE 124

1 There are many myths and misunderstandings surrounding the driving test.

Are the following true or false? Tick the correct boxes True False

1 The driving test is designed to see whether I can drive around a test route without making any mistakes. ☐ ☐

2 The driving test is designed to see whether I can drive safely under various traffic conditions. ☐ ☐

3 I do not need to know any of *The Highway Code*. ☐ ☐

4 The examiner has a set allocation of passes each week. ☐ ☐

5 I may be expected to drive up to the maximum national speed limit, where appropriate. ☐ ☐

2 The length of the normal driving test is approximately ...

1 60 minutes ☐

2 90 minutes ☐

3 40 minutes ☐

Tick the correct box

3 If, during the test, you do not understand what the examiner says to you, you would take a guess because you must not talk to him or her.

Is this statement true or false? True False

Tick the correct box ☐ ☐

SECTION 13

ANSWERS ON PAGE 124

4 You may have heard people say that it is easier to pass the driving test in certain parts of the country.

Do you agree with this statement?   Yes No

Tick the correct box   ☐ ☐

5 If you fail your test, you can take it again.

Which of the following statements is correct?

Tick the correct box(es)

1 If you fail the test, you can apply straight away for another appointment.   ☐

2 If you fail the test you have to wait a month before you can apply for another appointment.   ☐

3 You can re-take your test, subject to appointment availability, any time.   ☐

4 You have to wait 10 working days before you can re-take the test.   ☐

6 Before the practical part of your test, the examiner will test your eyesight.

This is done by asking you to read a number plate at a distance of ...

1 30.5 metres (100 feet)   ☐

2 20.5 metres (67 feet)   ☐

3 40.5 metres (133 feet)   ☐

Tick the correct box

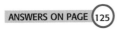
ANSWERS ON PAGE (125)

7 What will happen if you fail your eyesight test?

Answer _____

8 It is essential that you take both sections of your

p_ _ _ _ _ _ _ _ _ _ _ l_ _ _ _ _ to the test centre.
Complete the sentence

9 The examiner will expect you to drive without making any mistakes.

Do you think this statement is true or false?   True False
Tick the correct box   ☐   ☐

10 When reversing, are you allowed to undo your seat belt?   True False
Tick the correct box   ☐   ☐

11 If you fail your test, what will the examiner do?

1 _____

2 _____

12 When you have passed your driving test, what are you entitled to do?

1 _____

2 _____

3 _____

ANSWERS ON PAGE (125)

SECTION 13

13 I have within the last month passed my test.

Can I supervise a learner driver?

Tick the correct box

Yes   No
☐   ☐

14 When you have passed your test, what will the Examiner do with your provisional licence?

Answer _____

15 While you are waiting for your full licence to be sent to you, can you drive legally?

Tick the correct box

Yes   No
☐   ☐

16 It is recommended that you take further tuition once you have passed your test, especially on motorway driving.

As a learner driver you will not have experienced the special r__ __ __ __ that apply on the motorway and the h__ __ __ s__ __ __ __ of the other traffic.

Complete the sentence

ANSWERS ON PAGE (125)

17 While taking your driving test, you should drive ...

1 Especially carefully, keeping about 5mph below the speed limit ☐

2 As you would normally drive with your instructor ☐

3 With confidence, keeping at or just over the speed limit, to show that you can really drive ☐

Tick the correct box

18 Can you take a driving test if you are deaf?

Tick the correct box

Yes No
☐ ☐

ANSWERS ON PAGE 125

SECTION 13

The driving test ensures that all drivers reach a minimum standard.

1 Do you think that learning to drive ends with passing the test?

Tick the correct box

Yes No
☐ ☐

2 What knowledge and skills are not necessarily assessed in the present driving test?

List three

1 _____

2 _____

3 _____

3 Which of these statements do you think best describes advanced driving?

Tick the correct box

1 Advanced driving is learning to handle your car to its maximum performance. ☐

2 Advanced driving is learning to drive defensively with courtesy and consideration to others. ☐

3 Advanced driving is learning to drive fast. ☐

ANSWERS ON PAGE (125)

HINTS & TIPS

DRIVING IS A SKILL YOU CAN IMPROVE FOR THE REST OF YOUR LIFE; CONSIDER FURTHER TRAINING AFTER THE TEST.

SECTION 14

4 Some people have difficulty in driving at night.

Which age group would you expect, in general, to experience most difficulties?

Tick the correct box

1 Older people ☐

2 Younger people ☐

5 Once you have passed your driving test, your licence is usually valid until you reach __ __ years of age.

Complete the sentence

6 There are particular circumstances under which you are required to take a driving test again.

Name them

Answer _____

_____

7 Motorways are designed to enable traffic to travel faster in greater safety.

Compared to other roads, are they statistically ...

1 Safer? ☐

2 Less safe? ☐

3 No different? ☐

Tick the correct box

ANSWERS ON PAGE 125

8 **Are the following groups allowed on the motorway?**

1 Provisional licence holders ☐

2 Motor cycles over 50cc ☐

3 Pedestrians ☐

4 HGV learner drivers ☐

5 Newly qualified drivers with less than three months' experience ☐

6 Motor cycles under 125cc ☐

7 Cyclists ☐

Tick the correct box

9 **There are some routine checks you should carry out on your car before driving on the motorway.**

Name four of them

1 _____ 2 _____

3 _____ 4 _____

10 **On the motorway, if something falls from either your own or another vehicle, should you ...**

1 Flash your headlights to inform other drivers? ☐

2 Pull over, put your hazard warning lights on and quickly run on to the motorway to collect the object? ☐

3 Pull over on to the hard shoulder, use the emergency telephone to call the police? ☐

4 Flag another motorist down to get help? ☐

Tick the correct box

ANSWERS ON PAGE 125

11 Which colour do you associate with motorway signs?

1 Black lettering on a white background ☐

2 White lettering on a green background ☐

3 White lettering on a blue background ☐

Tick the correct box

12 At night or in poor weather conditions, your headlights will pick out reflective studs. Match the colour of the studs to their function by placing the appropriate letter in the box.

A AMBER   B RED   C GREEN   D WHITE

1 Marks the edge of the hard shoulder ☐

2 Marks the edge the central reservations ☐

3 Marks the lane lines ☐

4 Marks the exits and entrances ☐

13 Do the broken lines at the end of the acceleration lane mean ...

1 The edge of the carriageway? ☐

2 Other traffic should let you in? ☐

3 Give way to traffic already on the carriageway? ☐

Tick the correct box

SECTION 14

ANSWERS ON PAGE 126

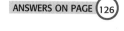

14 If you see congestion ahead, is it legal to use your hazard warning lights to warn drivers behind you?

Tick the correct box

Yes No

☐ ☐

15 What is the most common cause of accidents on motorways?

1 Vehicles breaking down ☐

2 Drivers falling asleep ☐

3 Drivers travelling too fast, too close to the vehicle in front ☐

4 Fog ☐

Tick the correct box

16 Are the following statements true or false?

I can use the hard shoulder ...

True False

1 To take a short break ☐ ☐

2 To stop and read a map ☐ ☐

3 To allow the children to stretch their legs ☐ ☐

4 To pull over in an emergency ☐ ☐

5 To answer a phone call ☐ ☐

Tick the correct box

ANSWERS ON PAGE 126

17 In normal driving on the motorway, you should overtake ...

1 On the right ☐

2 On the left ☐

3 On either side ☐

Tick the correct box

Driving at night can cause problems.

18 Which of these statements do you think is correct?

Tick the correct box

1 Street lighting and my car's headlights mean that I can see just as well as in the daylight. Therefore driving at night is just like driving in the daylight. ☐

2 At night I have to rely on my car's headlights and any additional lighting. Therefore I cannot see as far or drive as fast as in the daylight. ☐

19 At dusk and dawn what action should you take to compensate for driving a dark coloured car?

Answer _____

20 When driving after dark in a built-up area, should you use ...

1 Dipped headlights? ☐

2 Side or dim-dipped lights? ☐

Tick the correct box

SECTION 14

ANSWERS ON PAGE (126)

21 *The Highway Code* says you should not use your horn in a built-up area between 11.30pm and 7am.

What is the exception to that rule?

Answer _____

22 The diagram below illustrates two vehicles parked at night on a two-way road.

Which one is parked correctly?

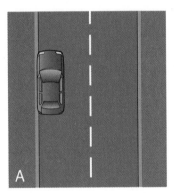 

23 Certain groups of road users are particularly vulnerable at night.

Name two of them

1 _____   2 _____

24 Under what circumstances would you use dipped headlights during the day?

Answer _____

S__ __ and b__ s__ __ __.   *Complete the sentence*

ANSWERS ON PAGE 126

25 When you are waiting at a junction after dark, your brake lights might

d_ _ _ _ _ the driver behind. It is better to use your

h_ _ _ _ _ _ _ _ _.

Complete the sentences

Certain weather conditions can create hazardous driving conditions in the summer as well as in the winter.

26 Which of the following causes greatest danger to drivers?

Tick the correct box

1 Snow ☐

2 Ice ☐

3 Heavy rain ☐

4 Not being able to see properly ☐

27 In wet weather conditions your tyres can lose their grip.

You should allow at least d_ _ _ _ _ the distance between you and the car in front that you allow on a dry road.

Fill in the missing word

28 In very wet conditions there is a danger of a build-up of water between your tyres and the road.

This is called a_ _ _ _ _ _ _ _ _ _ _.

Fill in the missing word

SECTION

14

ANSWERS ON PAGE (126)

29 How can you prevent a build-up of water occurring?

S_ _ _ d_ _ _ .

30 How should you deal with floods?

Tick the correct box

1 Drive through as fast as possible to avoid stopping ☐

2 Drive through slowly in 1st gear, slipping the clutch to keep the engine speed high ☐

3 Drive through in the highest gear possible, slipping the clutch to keep the engine speed high ☐

31 Will less tread on your tyres ...

1 Increase your braking distance? ☐

2 Decrease your braking distance? ☐

Tick the correct box

32 When the tyres lose contact with the road, the steering will feel v_ _ _ l_ _ _ _ _.

Complete the sentence

ANSWERS ON PAGE (126)

SECTION 14

33 After you have driven through a flood, should you check ...

1 Your speedometer?

2 Your brakes?

3 Your oil?

Tick the correct box

34 There are certain key precautions you should take when driving in fog.

Complete the following sentences

1 S__ __ __ d__ __ __.

2 Ensure you are able to s__ __ __ within the distance you can see to be clear.

3 Use your w__ __ __ __ __ __ __ __ __ __ w__ __ __ __ __.

4 Use your d__ __ __ __ __ __ __ and your h__ __ __ __ __ r__ __ __ w__ __ __ __ __ __ __ __ __.

35 Under what circumstances should you use your rear fog lights?

When visibility is less than _____ metres/yards

Fill in the correct number

36 When you are following another vehicle in fog, should you ...

1 Follow closely behind because it will help you see where you are going?

2 Leave plenty of room between you and the vehicle in front?

Tick the correct box

SECTION 14

ANSWERS ON PAGE (126)

 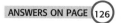

37 When you are following another vehicle in fog, should you use ...

   1 Main beam headlights?

   2 Dipped headlights?

   Tick the correct box

38 Extra precautions are needed when dealing with a junction in fog.

   Complete the following sentences

   1 Open your w__ __ __ __ __ __ and switch off your a__ __ __ __

      s__ __ __ __ __ __. L__ __ __ __ __ for other vehicles.

   2 Signal e__ __ __ __ .

   3 Use your b__ __ __ __ __. The light will a__ __ __ __ following vehicles.

   4 Use your h__ __ __ if you think it will w__ __ __ other road users.

39 Is the following statement about anti-lock brakes true or false?

   Anti-lock brakes will stop me skidding when driving on snow or ice.

   True **False**

   Tick the correct box

40 When driving in snow or ice you should gently test your

   b__ __ __ __ __ from time to time.

   Fill in the missing word

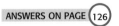

ANSWERS ON PAGE 126

41 In order to slow down when driving on snow or ice you should ...

1 Use your brakes g__ __ __ __ __ .

2 Get into a l__ __ __ __ g__ __ __ earlier than normal.

3 Allow your speed to d__ __ __ and use b__ __ __ __ __ gently and early.

Fill in the missing words

42 On snow or ice, braking distances can increase by ...

1 10 times ☐

2 5 times ☐

3 20 times ☐

4 15 times ☐

Tick the correct box

43 When going downhill in snow, what would you do to help you slow down?

*Answer*_____

44 When cornering in snow or ice, what should you avoid doing?

*Answer*_____

45 How can you reduce the risk of wheel spin?

*Answer*_____

SECTION

14

ANSWERS ON PAGE (126)

 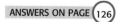

46 Three important factors cause a skid

Name them

1 _____

2 _____

3 _____

HINTS & TIPS

IF YOU REALISE THAT YOUR CAR IS STARTING TO SKID, EASE OFF THE BRAKE AND ACCELERATOR, THEN STEER SMOOTHLY IN THE SAME DIRECTION AS THE SKID.

47 Some everyday driving actions, especially in poor weather, can increase the risk of skidding.

Fill in the missing words

1 S_ _ _ _ _ _ down.

2 S_ _ _ _ _ _ _ up.

3 T_ _ _ _ _ _ corners.

4 Driving u_ _ _ _ _ and d_ _ _ _ _ _ _.

ANSWERS ON PAGE 126

All vehicles need routine attention and maintenance to keep them in good working order. Neglecting maintenance can be costly and dangerous.

1 With which of these statements do you agree?

Tick the correct box

1 Allowing the fuel gauge to drop too low is bad for the engine. ☐

2 In modern cars the fuel level makes little difference. ☐

2 What do you put into the engine to lubricate the moving parts?

Answer _____

3 How frequently should you check your oil level?

Tick the correct box

1 Once a month ☐

2 Once a year ☐

3 Every time you fill up with fuel ☐

4 The engine is often cooled by a mixture of w_ _ _ _ and

a_ _ _ _ f_ _ _ _ _ _. Some engines are a_ _ cooled.

Complete the sentence

5 How frequently should you test your brakes?

Tick the correct box

1 Daily ☐   3 Weekly ☐

2 Monthly ☐   4 When I use them ☐

6 Incorrectly adjusted headlamps can cause d_ _ _ _ _ to other road users.

Complete the sentence

7 All headlamps, indicators and brake lights should be kept in good working order.

It is also important that they are kept c_ _ _ _ .

Fill in the missing word

8 Tyres should be checked for u_ _ _ _ _ wear and tyre walls

for b_ _ _ _ _ and c_ _ _.

Complete the sentence

9 The legal requirement for tread depth is not less than ...

1 1.4mm ☐   2 1.6mm ☐   3 2mm ☐

Tick the correct box

SECTION

15

ANSWERS ON PAGE 127

10 What should you do if your brakes feel slack or spongy?

Answer _____

11 Vehicle breakdowns could result from ...

1 N_ _ _ _ _ _ of the vehicle

2 Lack of r_ _ _ _ _ _ _ c_ _ _ _ _

3 Little or no p_ _ _ _ _ _ _ _ _ _ _ _ maintenance

4 A_ _ _ _ of the vehicle

Fill in the missing words

12 It is advisable to carry a warning triangle.

1 On a straight road how far back should it be placed?

45 metres/yards ☐   200 metres/yards ☐   150 metres/yards ☐

Tick the correct box

2 On a dual carriageway, how far back should it be placed?
At least ...

200 metres/yards ☐   150 metres/yards ☐   450 metres/yards ☐

Tick the correct box

SECTION 15

ANSWERS ON PAGE 127

13 If you use a warning triangle, is it worth putting your hazard lights on as well?

Yes   No

Tick the correct box   ☐ ☐

14 If your vehicle breaks down on a motorway, should you ...

1 Gently brake, put your hazard lights on and seek assistance?   ☐

2 Pull over to the central reservation as far to the right as possible?   ☐

3 Pull over safely on to the hard shoulder as far away from the carriageway as possible?   ☐

Tick the correct box

15 If your vehicle has broken down on the motorway, should you tell your passengers to ...

1 Stay in the vehicle while you seek assistance?   ☐

2 Wait by the car on the hard shoulder but watch for other vehicles?   ☐

3 Get out of the vehicle and wait on the embankment away from the hard shoulder?   ☐

Tick the correct box

ANSWERS ON PAGE (127)

16 The marker posts at the side of all motorways have a picture of a telephone handset.

How can you tell which way to walk to reach the nearest telephone?

Answer _____

_____

_____

17 When you use the emergency telephone on a motorway, what will the operator ask you?

1 _____

2 _____

3 _____

4 _____

18 Disabled drivers cannot easily get to an emergency telephone. How can they summon help?

1 _____

2 _____

SECTION

15

ANSWERS ON PAGE 127

 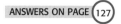

19 If you break down when travelling alone, there are three things you are advised NOT to do.

Complete the sentences

1 Do not ask p_ _ _ _ _ _ _ m_ _ _ _ _ _ _ _ _ for help.

2 Do not accept help from anyone you d_ n_ _ k_ _ _ (except the emergency services or a breakdown service).

3 Do not l_ _ _ _ _ you vehicle l_ _ _ _ _ than necessary.

20 If I am first or one of the first to arrive at the scene of an accident, should I ...

True False

1 Always move injured people away from vehicles? ☐ ☐

2 Tell the ambulance personnel or paramedics what I think is wrong with those injured? ☐ ☐

3 Give casualties something warm to drink? ☐ ☐

4 Switch off hazard warning lights? ☐ ☐

5 Switch off vehicle engines? ☐ ☐

6 Inform the police of the accident? ☐ ☐

Tick the correct boxes

ANSWERS ON PAGE (127)

21 If you are involved in an accident, what MUST you do?

Answer _____

22 If you are involved in an accident and nobody is injured, do you have to call the police?

Yes No

Tick the correct box ☐ ☐

SECTION 15

23 What information do you need to exchange if you are involved in an accident?

1 _____

2 _____

3 _____

4 _____

5 _____

24 If you thought you had a fire in your car's engine, what action would you take?

1 _____

2 _____

3 _____

25 There are three items of emergency equipment it is wise to carry in your car.

1 F_ _ _ _ _ A_ _ kit.

2 F_ _ _ e_ _ _ _ _ _ _ _ _ _ _ _.

3 W_ _ _ _ _ _ _ t_ _ _ _ _ _ _ _.

Fill in the missing words

SECTION

15

ANSWERS ON PAGE (127)

26 When you rejoin a motorway from the hard shoulder, should you ...

1 Signal right and join when there is safe gap? ☐

2 Keep your hazard lights on and drive down the hard shoulder until there is a safe gap? ☐

3 Use the hard shoulder to build up speed and join the carriageway when safe? ☐

Tick the correct box

27 Fuel combustion causes waste products.

One of these is a gas called c_ _ _ _ _ _ d_ _ _ _ _ _. This is

a major cause of the g_ _ _ _ _ _ _ _ _ _ effect.

Complete the sentences

28 How much does transport contribute to the production of carbon dioxide in the country (expressed as a percentage of the total production)?

1 10 per cent ☐

2 25 per cent ☐

3 50 per cent ☐

4 20 per cent ☐

Tick the correct box

ANSWERS ON PAGE (127)

SECTION 15

29 The MOT test checks the roadworthiness of a vehicle.

Does it include an exhaust emission test?

Tick the correct box

Yes No

☐ ☐

30 A catalytic convertor stops the emission of carbon dioxide.

Tick the correct box

True False

☐ ☐

31 Which uses up more fuel?

1 A car travelling at 50mph ☐

2 A car travelling at 70mph ☐

Tick the correct box

32 There are some measures car drivers can take to help reduce damage to the environment.

List five

1 _____

2 _____

3 _____

4 _____

5 _____

SECTION

15

ANSWERS ON PAGE 127

 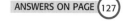

Before buying a used car it is best to decide what you want the car for and how much you can afford.

33 There are three main sources of supply for used vehicles.

You can buy from a d_ _ _ _ _, at an a_ _ _ _ _ _ or

p_ _ _ _ _ _ _ _.

Complete the sentence

34 When reading a glowing description of a used car, what should you first consider?

Answer _____

35 Are these statements about buying a used car through a dealer or at an auction true or false?

		True	False
1	It is often cheaper to buy a car at an auction than through a dealer.	☐	☐
2	I have the same legal rights when I buy at an auction as when I buy from a dealer.	☐	☐
3	I should always read the terms and conditions of trade before I buy a car at an auction.	☐	☐
4	The best way to select a used car dealer is by recommendation.	☐	☐

Tick the correct boxes

ANSWERS ON PAGE 127

SECTION

15

36 Cars bought through a dealer often have a warranty.

What should you check?

1 _____

2 _____

37 When you test drive a vehicle, you should make sure that it is t__ __ __ __,

has a current M__ __ certificate (if applicable) and that

all i__ __ __ __ __ __ __ __ requirements are complied with.

Complete the sentence

38 There are some important items that you should check on before you buy a used car.

List three

1 _____

2 _____

3 _____

39 Do you think the following statement is true or false?

It is advisable to have my vehicle examined by a competent and unbiased expert before I buy.

True False

☐ ☐

Tick the correct box

SECTION

15

ANSWERS ON PAGE 128

 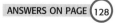

Particular difficulties are encountered when towing a caravan or trailer. There are some very good courses which will help master the skills required.

1 People can underestimate the length of the total combination of car and caravan or trailer.

Is the overall length usually ...

1 Twice the length of a normal car?

2 Three times the length of a normal car?

Tick the correct box

2 What additional fixtures should you attach to your car to help you see more clearly?

Answer _____

3 When towing you will need more distance than normal to overtake. Is it ...

1 Twice the normal distance?

2 Three times the normal distance?

3 Four times the normal distance?

Tick the correct box

4 A device called a s_ _ _ _ _ _ _ _ _ will make the combination safer to handle.

Fill in the missing word

SECTION

16

ANSWERS ON PAGE (128)

5 The stability of the caravan will depend on how you load it.
Should heavy items be loaded ...

☐ **1** At the front? ☐ **2** At the rear? ☐ **3** Over the axle(s)?

Tick the correct box

6 There are special restrictions for vehicles which are towing.

A What is the speed limit on a dual carriageway?

Tick the correct box

☐ **1** 50mph ☐ **2** 60mph ☐ **3** 70mph

B What is the speed on a single carriageway?

Tick the correct box

☐ **1** 40mph ☐ **2** 50mph ☐ **3** 60mph

7 There are some important checks you should make before starting off.

List four

1 _____ 2 _____

3 _____ 4 _____

8 If you decide to stop to take a break, before allowing anyone to enter
the caravan you should lower the j_ _ _ _ _ _ w_ _ _ _ _ and

c_ _ _ _ _ s_ _ _ _ _ _ _ _.

Fill in the missing words

ANSWERS ON PAGE 128

SECTION 16

Many people now take their car abroad or hire a vehicle when on holiday.

9 Motoring organisations, such as The Automobile Association, can help you plan and organise your trip.

The AA can provide advice on travel and v_ _ _ _ _ _ insurance.

They will also help you organise the d_ _ _ _ _ _ _ _ _ that you will need.

Fill in the missing words

10 Before travelling to Europe, you should always ...

1 Plan the r_ _ _ _ you wish to take.

2 Know the local m_ _ _ _ _ _ _ _ r_ _ _ _ _ _ _ _ _ _ _ _.

Complete the sentences

11 It is essential that your vehicle should be checked thoroughly.

List four of the routine checks you should make

1 _____

2 _____

3 _____

4 _____

ANSWERS ON PAGE (128)

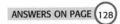

12 In most European countries you are advised to carry your

d_ _ _ _ _ _ _   l_ _ _ _ _ _ _   on you.

Complete the sentence

13 What do the letters IDP stand for?

Answer _____

14 Where might you need an IDP?

Answer _____

15 In most European countries what age do you have to be to drive?

1 ☐   21   2 ☐   18   3 ☐   16

Tick the correct box

16 Some European countries can require you to carry additional emergency equipment.

List four of the items you are recommended to carry

1 _____

2 _____

3 _____

4 _____

SECTION

16

ANSWERS ON PAGE (128)

Now you are the proud possessor of a full driving licence which allows you to drive vehicles up to 3.5 tonnes, use motorways for the first time, drive anywhere in the European Union and in many other countries worldwide, and to tow a small trailer. You are on your own dealing with whatever circumstances arise: fog, snow, ice, other drivers' mistakes. It is a huge responsibility.

Gaining experience is the key to a safe driving career. A new driver is at greater risk in the first two years following their test than at any other time. It is because of this that licence regulations stipulate that the accumulation of six or more penalty points during the first two years will mean the loss of a full driving licence and reversion to provisional status. This means that both theory and practical tests will have to be taken and passed all over again.

Having passed the driving test doesn't mean you have learnt everything there is to know; you will continue learning for the rest of your life. Consider some further training – this time without the comfort of L plates.

PASS PLUS

The Driving Standards Agency and the insurance industry recognise and seek to reward those new drivers who enhance their basic skills and widen their experience by taking further training in the form of the Pass Plus scheme.

This is a six-module syllabus which covers town and rural driving, night driving, driving in adverse conditions and motorway experience. An increasing number of insurance companies are prepared to offer discounts to new drivers who have completed the course.

Consider what real driving is all about; compare it to the type of driving you did when learning. There is little similarity. Your lesson is likely to have been about two hours long including stops for explanations, and you knew you could always fall back on the support of your instructor. Everyday driving involves driving in different areas, perhaps for extended periods, with only your own decisions to rely on.

SECTION 17

Pass Plus provides a half-way solution. You have the benefit of your instructor's presence in a car you are familiar with, but this time in situations you are unfamiliar with, and with no L plates. It provides you with an opportunity to gain controlled experience.

MOTORWAY DRIVING

People learn to drive for a huge variety of reasons, but one reason that crops up time and time again is the freedom it allows. You will limit that freedom if you do not include the use of motorways as part of your experience. As a minimum but essential topic, you should have a lesson with your instructor on motorway driving, as this is the one road situation where up to now your training could not take place.

Contrary to popular belief, motorways are very safe roads when used properly. Only about 4% of accidents occur on motorways compared to 70% in urban areas. Learn how to use them safely.

You will have already realised that the faster you drive, the faster you must think and be able to react. Motorways are faster roads, so you must develop greater observation, anticipation and planning skills. Because you are effectively driving on a one-way road often for long distances and durations, levels of concentration must also be maintained.

The maximum speed on a motorway is 70mph; this is a maximum not a target. Even though some drivers ignore this limit, you must not be pulled along by other traffic into dangerous and illegal situations. Drive at a speed with which you are comfortable, but recognise that it would also be dangerous to hinder the progress of others.

Joining and leaving motorways are often the situations that less experienced drivers find most daunting. You already know the theory and the rules, but they have to be put into practice. The first time you do this on your own, make sure it is on a quiet stretch of motorway. Leave at the very next exit and rejoin immediately; this will build up your experience much more quickly.

SECTION

17

Boredom and fatigue can also affect safe driving on motorways. Do not drive for a long time without taking a break. In the early stages 'a long time' may be a mere half-hour, but even when you become more experienced, the time between breaks should not be more than two hours.

It is estimated that a high percentage of motorway accidents can be attributed to fatigue, and worse still, to falling asleep. Excluding those with sleep disorders, people know when they are tired or fighting sleep. This is not the time to carry on driving. Take a break, take a nap.

YOU – THE CAR – THE ENVIRONMENT

Owning and running a car is an expensive business. The cost is not just measured in the price of the fuel you buy, but in the wider consequences of cost to the environment. Every driver can take some simple actions which will help everyone.

On a daily basis ask yourself: do you really need to make that short car journey? Once a week check that tyres are correctly inflated; not only will wrong pressures wear the tyres more quickly, but under-inflation will increase fuel consumption.

Look after the vehicle you drive, make sure it is serviced regularly and the engine correctly tuned. Not only will this help to keep pollution to a minimum but also to make sure fuel is burnt efficiently. Remove excess weight from your vehicle; even an empty roof rack will increase fuel consumption by about 5%.

The way you drive also affects the volume of fuel that the engine burns. By driving smoothly and avoiding sudden acceleration or braking, fuel is not wasted and you and your passengers have a more comfortable ride. By driving at 70mph up to 30% more fuel would be used than driving at 50mph. Use speed appropriately and economically. See pages 138–143 for more information.

SECTION 17

Section 1

INTRODUCTION TO LEARNING TO DRIVE
Questions on pages 12–13

A1
A current, signed, full or provisional licence for the category of vehicle that you are driving

A2
examinations
register

A3
21 years old
three years

A4
To the front and rear. It is important not to place them in windows where they could restrict good vision.

A5
True

A6
You should have answered No to all the questions.

A7
Yes. This should be the ambition of every driver.

A8 3, 4

ADJUSTING YOUR DRIVING POSITION
Questions on page 14

A9
1 handbrake
2 doors
3 seat
4 head restraint
5 mirrors
6 seat belt

INTRODUCTION TO VEHICLE CONTROLS
Questions on pages 14–15

A10
The handbrake	E
The driving mirrors	D
The gear lever	F
The clutch	G
The steering wheel	A
The foot-brake	B
The accelerator	C

A11
The foot-brake	R
The clutch	L
The accelerator	R

A12
1 False. You will need one hand to change gear or use other controls.
2 True
3 False. The best position is quarter to three or ten to two.
4 False. It is safest to feed the wheel through your hands.
5 True
6 True

A13
The direction indicators	B
Dipped beam	A
Main beam	D
Rear fog lamp	C
Horn	E
Hazard lights	F

Section 2

MOVING OFF
Questions on page 16

A1
A	1
B	5
C	3
D	2

E	6
F	4
G	7
H	8
I	9

STOPPING (NORMALLY)
Questions on page 17

A2
A	1
B	3
C	2
D	4
E	6
F	5
G	8
H	7
I	9

GEAR CHANGING
Questions on pages 18–20

A3
1st gear

A4
5th, or 4th if the car has a 4-speed gear box

A5
Usually 2nd gear, but 1st if you need to go very slowly or 3rd if the corner is sweeping and you can take it safely at a higher speed

A6
engine
vehicle
sound
when

A7
A	1
B	3
C	2
D	4
E	5

A8
1 False. This will cause the engine to labour.
2 False. It is good practice to use the brakes to slow the car down. Using the transmission causes wear and tear which can be very costly. Also, the brakes are more effective.
3 False
4 True
5 False. It is good practice to miss out the unwanted gears and select the gear most appropriate to your road speed.

A9
1

A10
1 Don't
2 Don't
3 Do
4 Do
5 Do
6 Don't
7 Don't
8 Don't

STEERING
Questions on page 21

A11
A, except in a few cars fitted with four-wheel steering (in which case all four wheels will move)

A12
A

A13
B

A14
B

ROAD POSITIONING
Questions on page 22

A15
C well to the left but not too close to the kerb

A16
B. Avoid swerving in and out. It is unnecessary and confuses other drivers.

CLUTCH CONTROL
Questions on page 23

A17
A

A18
biting

A19
1 Yes
2 Yes
3 No
4 Yes
5 No

Section 3

JUNCTIONS
Questions on pages 24–7

A1
two or more roads

A2
A T-junction
B Y-junction
C Roundabout
D Staggered crossroads
E Crossroads

A3
1 E
2 C
3 B
4 D
5 A

A4
A 1
B 3

A5
1 Mirrors
2 Signal
3 Position

4 Speed
5 Look

A6
assess
decide
act

A7
A

A8
B

A9
D

A10
1 mirrors, position
2 signal
3 safe
4 safe distance
5 overtake

CROSSROADS
Questions on page 28

A11
A 3 Crossroads. Priority for traffic on the major road. Never assume other drivers will give you priority.
B 1 Unmarked crossroads
C 2 Crossroads with give way lines at the end of your road. Give way to traffic on the major road.

ROUNDABOUTS
Questions on pages 29–31

A12
C

A13
1 Left
2 Left
3 Right. Remember to use the MSM routine before signalling left to turn off.

A14
1 Left

2 Going ahead
3 Right

A15
mirrors
signal
position
speed
look

A16 2

Section 4

PARKING (ON THE ROAD)
Questions on pages 32–3

A1
1 safe
2 considerate
3 legal

A2
Cars 1, 2, 3, 6

A3
1 False
2 False
3 True
4 True

A4
Any of the following:
at a bus stop
at a school entrance
opposite a junction
on a bend
on the brow of a hill
on a Clearway
on a motorway
at night facing oncoming traffic
in a residents' parking zone.

Section 5

PASSING STATIONARY VEHICLES AND OBSTRUCTIONS
Questions on page 34

A1
Vehicle 2

A2
Vehicle 2, even though the obstruction is on the right. Where safe, when travelling downhill be prepared to give priority to vehicles (especially heavy vehicles) that are coming uphill.

MEETING AND CROSSING THE PATH OF OTHER VEHICLES
Questions on pages 35–6

A3
1 True
2 False. Always consider whether it is safe. Are there dangers the other driver cannot see? Remember, flashing headlamps has the same meaning as sounding the horn. It is a warning: 'I am here!' Sometimes it is taken to mean: 'I am here and I am letting you pass.'
3 True

A4
1 Yes
2 Yes
3 No
4 Yes
5 Yes
6 Yes
7 Yes

Section 6

STOPPING IN AN EMERGENCY
Questions on pages 37–8

A1
1 True
2 True
3 True

4 False. Looking in the mirror should not be necessary. You should know what is behind you.
5 False
6 True
7 True

A2
False. An emergency stop will be conducted randomly on only some tests. You must always know how to stop safely in an emergency.

A3
pump
1 maximum
2 lock
3 quickly

A4
steer
brake
pump
pressure

1 False. Other elements beyond braking can cause skidding e.g. acceleration or going too fast into a bend.
2 False. Although you may stop in a shorter distance, you still need to leave the correct distance to allow yourself time to react and vehicles behind you time to stop.

STOPPING DISTANCES
Questions on pages 39–40

A5
1 No
2 Yes
3 Yes
4 No

A6 ½ second

A7
1 23 metres/75 feet
2 15 metres/50 feet
3 96 metres/315 feet

A8
longer
more

A9
breaks
two-second

Section 7

MOVING OFF AT AN ANGLE
Question on page 41

A1
1 False. You should check your mirrors and blindspot before moving out. Keep alert for other traffic as you pull out and stop if necessary.
2 True
3 False. Move out slowly and carefully.
4 True. The closer you are, the greater the angle.
5 True. As you move out, you are likely to move on to the right-hand side of the road and into conflict with oncoming vehicles.
6 False. You should signal only if it helps or warns other road users. Signalling gives you no right to pull out.

MOVING OFF UPHILL
Question on page 42

A2
1 True
2 False. Using the accelerator pedal will not move the car forwards.

3 False. As your feet will be using the clutch pedal and the accelerator pedal you need to use the handbrake to stop the car rolling back.
4 True
5 True
6 True
7 True

MOVING OFF DOWNHILL
Question on page 43

A3
1 True
2 False. Almost certainly you will need to use the foot-brake.
3 False. It is often better to move off in 2nd gear.
4 True. This will stop the car rolling forwards.
5 True
6 False. You will need to have your foot on the foot-brake to stop the car rolling forwards.

APPROACHING JUNCTIONS UPHILL AND DOWNHILL
Question on page 44

A4
The following statements are correct:
1, 4, 5, 6, 7

Section 8

REVERSING
Questions on pages 45–7

A1
safe
convenient
law

A2
1 False
2 False

3 True
4 True

A3 A

A4 1, 4

A5
Car A: to the left
Car B: to the right

A6
observation

REVERSING INTO A SIDE ROAD ON THE LEFT
Questions on pages 47–8

A7 3

A8
1 True
2 False
3 True

A9 4

A10 C

A11 Left

A12
The front of the car will swing out to the right

A13
1 True
2 False
3 True

A14
pedestrians
road users
stop

REVERSING INTO A SIDE ROAD ON THE RIGHT
Questions on pages 49–50

A15 True

A16 B

A17 2

A18
True. You may need to place your left hand at 12 o'clock and lower your right hand.

A19 True

A20 2

A21 B

TURNING IN THE ROAD
Questions on pages 51–3

A22 A

A23
slowly
briskly

A24
False, but you should try to complete the manoeuvre in as few moves as possible.

A25 2, 3, 4

A26
all round

A27
1 Right
2 Steer briskly left
3 Left
4 Steer briskly right
5 Right

A28
1 Left
2 Over your right shoulder to where the car is going

REVERSE PARALLEL PARKING
Questions on pages 54–7

A29 2

A30
C, in line with the rear of the parked vehicle

A31 2

A32
1 To the left
2 The nearside headlamp of the vehicle towards which you are reversing
3 Clipping the rear offside of the lead car
4 Take off the left lock
5 Steer to the right and then take off the right lock as you get straight

A33
1 False
2 False
3 True. You will be expected to be able to complete the exercise within approximately two car lengths.

A34
All round, particularly for pedestrians and oncoming vehicles

A35
C. The other bay widths are reduced by parked vehicles. This may make opening doors a squeeze.

A36
Allows you to make best use of the area in front of the bay
Gives you a better view when driving out of the space

A37
close
directions
pedestrians

Section 9

TRAFFIC LIGHTS AND YELLOW BOX JUNCTIONS
Questions on pages 58–60

A1
1 red
2 red and amber
3 green
4 amber
5 red

A2
1 green
2 red and amber
3 amber
4 red

A3
1 False
2 True
3 True
4 False.
Pedestrians who are already crossing have priority.

A4 2

A5
1 Lane A or B
2 Lane C
3 Lane A

A6
1 No ⎤
2 No ⎦ If your exit is blocked you should not enter a yellow box junction.

3 Yes

 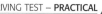

ANSWERS

PEDESTRIAN CROSSINGS
Questions on pages 60–3

A7
1 Zig-zag lines
2 Flashing yellow beacons on both sides of the road
3 Black and white stripes on the crossing
4 A give way line

A8
1 True
2 True. You must not park or wait on the zig-zag lines on either side of the crossing.
3 False. You must not overtake on the zig-zag lines on approach to the crossing.
4 True
5 True. A slowing down arm signal should be used. It helps pedestrians understand what you intend to do. They cannot see your brake lights.

A9
1 Traffic lights
2 Zig-zag lines
3 A white stop line

A10
2 A white stick means the pedestrian is visually impaired. A white stick with two reflector bands means the pedestrian may be deaf as well as visually impaired.

A11
1 Flashing amber
2 You must give way to pedestrians on the crossing, but if it is clear you may go on.

A12
A bleeping tone. This sounds when the red light shows to drivers and helps visually impaired pedestrians know when it is safe to cross.

A13
There is no flashing amber light sequence. The light sequence is the same as normal traffic lights.

A14 cyclists

LEVEL CROSSINGS
Questions on page 63

A15

A	3
B	1
C	2
D	4

A16
2
4
5

Section 10

ONE-WAY SYSTEMS
Questions on page 64

A1
A is the correct sign for a one-way street.
B tells you 'Ahead only'.

A2
1 True
2 True
3 True
4 True

ROAD MARKINGS
Questions on pages 64–7

A3
information
warnings
orders

A4
1 They can be seen when other signs may be hidden
2 They give a continuing message

A5

A 2
B 2

A6
1, 4

A7
They are used to separate potentially dangerous streams of traffic.

A8
You must not enter the hatched area.

TRAFFIC SIGNS
Questions on pages 67–8

A9
1 Warning
2 Order
3 Information

A10
1 must
2 must not

A11
1 You must give way to traffic on the major road. Delay your entry until it is safe to join the major road.
2 You must stop (even if the road is clear). Wait until you can enter the new road safely.

A12
vision is limited

A13
Motorway signs   D
Primary routes   E

Other routes	B
Local places	C
Tourist signs	A

Section 11

ROAD OBSERVATION
Questions on pages 69–71

A1
speed
behaviour
intentions

A2
1 Observe that the view into the new road is restricted.
The driver should ...
Move forward slowly, to get a better view.
Note the pedestrian who may walk in front of or behind car A.
Note the pedestrian waiting to cross.
Allow the cyclist to pass.
Once in position to see car B, stop and give way.
2 Observe that the parked car restricts the view into and out of the side road.
The driver should ...
Slow down on approach to parked car P.
Take up position to gain a better view and be more visible to car A and the pedestrian.
Slow down in case the pedestrian walks out from behind the parked car P.
Consider signal to pass parked car P.
Look carefully into minor road. Note the actions of car A. Be prepared to stop.

A3 bike

A4 3

A5
A
1 Junctions
2 Hump-back bridges
3 Concealed entrances
4 Dead ground
5 Narrow lanes

B
1 Children playing
2 Horses
3 Pedestrians
4 Especially elderly and young cyclists
5 Other vehicles

A6
1 True. The ability to advise those at your destination of delays can help to reduce the worry of late arrivals
2 True
3 True
4 True

A7
All are distracting and upset concentration, and should not be carried out while driving.

DEALING WITH BENDS
Questions on pages 71–2

A8
speed
gear
position

A9 1

A10 B

A11 A

A12
A On a right-hand bend keep to the left. This will help to improve your view.
B On a left-hand bend keep to the centre of the lane. Do not move to the centre of the road to get a better view. A vehicle travelling in the opposite direction may be taking the bend wide.

OVERTAKING
Questions on pages 73–4

A13
necessary
1 Mirrors
2 Position
3 Speed
4 Look
5 Mirrors
6 Signal
7 Manoeuvre

A14
About the width of a small car, more in windy or poor weather conditions

A15
1 The vehicle in front is signalling and positioned to turn right
2 You are using the correct lane to turn left at a junction
3 Traffic is moving slowly in queues and the traffic on the right is moving more slowly than you are
4 You are in a one-way street

A16
1 On approach to a junction
2 The brow of a hill
3 The approach to a bend
4 Where there is dead ground. NB These are examples. Be guided by *The Highway Code*.

ANSWERS
18

DUAL CARRIAGEWAYS
Questions on pages 74–6

A17
2. Statements 1, 3, 4 and 5 do not apply:
1 Reflective studs are used on some dual carriageways.
3 The speed limit is subject to local conditions and may vary from 40mph up to the national speed limit.
4 You can turn right on to and off dual carriageways unlike motorways, where all traffic enters and leaves on the left.
5 You may find slow moving vehicles sometimes displaying a flashing amber light.

A18
A You would cross over the first carriageway then wait in the gap in the central reservation. Be careful, if you are towing or if your vehicle is long, that you do not cause other road users to change course or slow down.
B You would wait until there is a gap in the traffic long enough for you safely to clear the first carriageway and emerge into the second.

A19
The speed limit applies to all lanes. Use the first lane to travel in and the second for overtaking.

A20
A Dual carriageway ends
B Road narrows on both sides
C Two-way traffic straight ahead

A21
A and C

A22
Traffic is moving much faster, and one or more lanes will have to be crossed.

Section 12

DRIVING AN AUTOMATIC CAR
Questions on pages 77–80

A1
Clutch

A2
1 Driving is easier
2 There is more time to concentrate on the road

A3
Park – Locks the transmission. This should be selected only when the vehicle is stationary.
Reverse – Enables the car to go backwards, as in a manual car.
Neutral – Has the same function as in a manual car. The engine is not in contact with the driving wheels.
Drive – Is used for driving forwards. It automatically selects the most appropriate gear.
3rd
2nd } Have the same function as manual gears
1st

A4 3

A5
1 Yes
2 No
3 Yes, if you needed extra control
4 You would probably use kickdown, but possibly in certain circumstances you would manually select a lower gear
5 Yes, maybe using 1st gear
6 No. Use the brakes

A6
1 The right foot
2 The right foot

A7
It stops you trying to control the brake and accelerator at the same time. It encourages early release of the accelerator and progressive braking.

A8
Drive, reverse, all forward gears.

A9
1 You should apply the handbrake every time you stop. Otherwise you have to keep your foot on the foot-brake.

A10
Park (P) or Neutral (N)

A11 1

Section 13

THE DRIVING TEST
Questions on pages 81–5

A1
1 False
2 True
3 False
4 False
5 True

A2 3

A3
False. If you did not hear clearly or did not understand what the examiner said, you should ask him or her to repeat the instruction. If you have any problem with your hearing, it is advisable to tell the examiner at the start of the test.

A4
No. The standard test does not vary. The test result should be the same wherever it is taken.

A5
1, 4

A6
2

A7
The test will not proceed. You have failed not only the eyesight section, but the whole test. Remember, if you wear glasses or contact lenses, to wear them for the eyesight test and for the rest of the driving test.

A8
provisional licence

A9
False. You can make some less serious faults and still reach the required standard.

A10
Yes, but remember to do it up again when you have completed the exercise.

A11
1 Give you a verbal explanation of the main reasons for failure
2 Write out a form for you to take away showing you your main errors

A12
1 Drive unsupervised
2 Drive on a motorway
3 Drive without L-plates

A13
No. You must have had at least three years' driving experience (and be over 21 years of age).

A14
The Examiner will keep your provisional licence and arrange for DVLA to send your full licence to you.

A15
Yes. It is a good idea to keep a note of your driver number and the date you passed your test.

A16
rules
high speed

A17
2 The examiner will expect you to drive normally. You should abide by all speed limits and drive according to road and traffic conditions.

A18
Yes. The examiner will be skilled in giving instructions and directions to deaf candidates.

Section 14

BEYOND THE TEST
Questions on pages 86–7

A1
No

A2
1 Bad weather driving
2 Night-time driving
3 Motorway driving
4 Skid control ... and more

A3
2

A4
1, although people of any age can find it difficult to drive at night

A5
70

A6
There are certain serious driving offences which carry the penalty of disqualification. In order to regain a full licence, the disqualified driver has to apply for a provisional licence and take an extended test. If, because of certain illnesses, you have been unable to drive for 10 years, you will be required to take the test again in order to gain a full licence.
For new drivers: the accumulation of six or more penalty points within two years of passing the test will mean reverting to a provisional licence and re-sitting the test.

MOTORWAY DRIVING
Questions on pages 87–91

A7
1

A8
1 No
2 Yes
3 No
4 Yes
5 Yes
6 Yes
7 No

A9
1 Oil
2 Water
3 Fuel
4 Tyre pressures
These are just some of the checks; for more information, refer to your car's manual.

A10
3 You should never attempt to retrieve anything from the carriageway.

A11 3

A12
B Amber
A Red
D Green
C White

A13 3

A14 Yes

A15 3

A16
1 False
2 False
3 False
4 True
5 False

A17
1, except when traffic is moving slowly in queues and the queue on the right is travelling more slowly

SAFE NIGHT DRIVING
Questions on pages 91–3

A18 2

A19
Switch on earlier, switch off later.

A20
1. It helps others to see you.

A21
If you are stationary, to avoid danger from a moving vehicle.

A22
A. Always park with the flow of traffic. You will show red reflectors to vehicles travelling in your direction.

A23
1 Pedestrians
2 Cyclists   } two of these
3 Motor cyclists

A24
In poor weather conditions – see and be seen

A25
dazzle
handbrake

ALL-WEATHER DRIVING
Questions on pages 93–98

A26 4

A27
double

A28
aquaplaning

A29
Slow down
Allow time for the tread patterns to disperse the water.

A30 2

A31 1

A3 very light

A33 2

A34
1 Slow down
2 stop
3 windscreen wipers
4 demister, heated rear windscreen

A35
100 metres/yards

A36 2

A37 2

A38
1 windows, audio system. Listen
2 early
3 brakes, alert
4 horn, warn

A39
False, because your tyres are not in contact with the road

A40
brakes

A41
1 gently
2 lower gear
3 drop, brakes

A42 1

A43
If possible, control your speed before reaching the hill. Select a low gear early.

A44
Using your brakes

A45
Avoid harsh acceleration

A46
1 The driver
2 The vehicle
3 The road conditions

A47
1 Slowing
2 Speeding
3 Turning
4 uphill, downhill

ANSWERS

Section 15

VEHICLE CARE
Questions on pages 99–100

A1 1

A2 Oil

A3 3

A4
Water, anti-freeze, air

A5 1

A6
dazzle

A7
clean

A8
uneven, bulges, cuts

A9 2

A10
Get them checked as quickly as possible

BREAKDOWNS, ACCIDENTS AND EMERGENCIES
Questions on pages 101–6

A11
1 Neglect
2 routine checks
3 preventative
4 abuse

A12
1 45 metres/yards
2 At least 150 metres/yards

A13
Yes. Try to give as much warning as possible.

A14 3

A15 3

A16
Under the drawing of the handset is an arrow which points to the nearest telephone.

A17
1 The emergency number (painted on the box)
2 Vehicle details (make, registration mark, colour)
3 Membership details of your motoring organisation
4 Details of the fault

A18
1 By displaying a Help pennant
2 By using a mobile telephone

A19
1 passing motorists
2 do not know
3 leave, longer

A20
1 False. Do not move injured people unless they are in danger.
2 False. Tell them the facts, not what you think is wrong.
3 False. Do not give those injured anything to eat or drink. Keep them warm and reassure them.
4 False. Keep hazard lights on to warn other drivers.
5 True. Switch off engines. Put out cigarettes.
6 True, in the case of injury.

A21
Stop

A22 No

A23
1 The other driver's name, address and contact number
2 The registration numbers of all vehicles involved
3 The make of the other car
4 The other driver's insurance details
5 If the driver is not the owner, the owner's details.

A24
1 Pull up quickly
2 Get all passengers out
3 Call assistance

A25
1 First aid
2 Fire extinguisher
3 Warning triangle

A26 3

THE MOTOR CAR AND THE ENVIRONMENT
Questions on pages 106–7

A27
carbon dioxide, greenhouse

A28 4

A29 Yes

A30
False. A catalytic convertor reduces the level of carbon monoxide, nitrogen oxide and hydrocarbons by up to 90 per cent. Carbon dioxide is still produced.

A31 2

A32
Eight measures are listed here:
1 Make sure your vehicle is in good condition and regularly serviced.
2 Make sure tyres are correctly inflated. Under-inflated tyres waste fuel.

ANSWERS 18

3 Avoid harsh braking.
4 Buy a fuel-efficient vehicle.
5 Use the most appropriate gear.
6 Use your accelerator sensibly and avoid harsh acceleration.
7 Use unleaded fuel.
8 Dispose of waste oil, old batteries and used tyres sensibly.

BUYING A USED CAR
Questions on pages 108–9

A33
dealer, auction, privately

A34
Why is it being sold?

A35
1 True
2 False
3 True
4 True

A36
1 What is covered
2 The length of the agreement

A37
taxed, MOT, insurance

A38
Four items to check are listed here:
1 Mileage
2 Has it been involved in any accidents?
3 Number of owners
4 Is there any hire purchase or finance agreement outstanding?

A39
True. The AA offer a national inspection scheme.

Section 16

TOWING A CARAVAN OR TRAILER
Questions on pages 110–11

A1 1

A2
Exterior towing mirrors, to give you a good view

A3 2

A4
stabiliser

A5 3

A6
A 2
B 2

A7
Seven checks are listed here:
1 Is the caravan or trailer loaded correctly?
2 Is it correctly hitched up to your vehicle?
3 Are the lights and indicators working properly?
4 Is the braking system working correctly?
5 Is the jockey wheel assembly fully retracted?
6 Are tyre pressures correct?
7 Are all windows, doors and roof lights closed?

A8
jockey wheel, corner steadies

DRIVING IN EUROPE
Questions on pages 112–3

A9
vehicle, documents

A10
1 route
2 motoring regulations

A11
Here are five routine checks:
1 Tyres, including spare. Always carry a spare tyre.
2 Tool kit and jack.
3 Lamps and brake lights.
4 Fit deflectors to your headlamps to prevent dazzle to other drivers approaching on the left.
5 Check you have an extra exterior mirror on the left.

A12
driving licence

A13
International Driving Permit

A14
Some non-EU countries

A15 2

A16
Five items are listed here:
1 Spare lamps and bulbs
2 Warning triangle
3 First aid kit
4 Fire extinguisher
5 Emergency windscreen

LOOKING AFTER YOUR CAR

Once you've passed your test, you'll need to take proper care of your vehicle. This section is devoted to handy motoring tips that will help you learn to look after your car and save money on maintenance and servicing. Much of it is common sense but essential if you want to become a responsible and effective driver.

CONTENTS

Making Regular Checks

It's always worth checking your car regularly for wear and tear, especially at the start of a long journey. Getting your car serviced regularly in accordance with the manufacturer's schedule will help reduce the risk of breakdown.

There are also some easy checks that you can make yourself – a bit of preventative care always helps.

PREVENTATIVE CHECKS

Refer to your manual for the specific requirements of your vehicle. The following points are some of the most common and useful checks you can make.

- **Wheels and tyres** – Check your tyres including the spare. Look out for cuts and other damage, and monitor the general wear and state of the tread. The correct tyre pressure is important for tyre wear, fuel economy and vehicle handling. The legal limit on tyre tread depth is 1.6mm but performance is affected below

3mm, particularly in the wet. Replace tyres at 3mm to ensure you stay safe and within the law. Check tyre pressures regularly and before long journeys. Under-inflated tyres create more rolling resistance and so use more fuel. Getting tyre pressures right is important for safety. Refer to the car's handbook as pressures will normally have to be increased for heavier loads.

- **Fuel** – Try to avoid the possibility of running out of fuel. If you do let your car run on empty, there's a risk of damage and it may start picking up sludge or debris from the bottom of the tank.

- **Lights** – Check all lights at least once a week and replace any dead bulbs immediately. Get a friend to stand outside the vehicle and check all the lights work, including brakes, indicators, fog lamp, headlights and side lights, hazard and number plate lights. Some modern headlight bulbs will require a visit to a garage for replacement.

● **Fluids** – Don't forget to check your engine oil, coolant, brake fluid and washer fluid levels regularly and top up if necessary. Check the vehicle's handbook carefully to make sure you use the right fluids in the right place as adding water to the engine or braking system will result in expensive damage. Also look for any leaks, if there is one you'll be able to spot the tell-tale drips under the car or stains on the driveway.

● **Windscreen wipers** – Worn or damaged windscreen wipers will make vision worse rather than better. Renew your wiper blades once a year. Spring is the best time as damage is more likely during the winter.

● **Fan belt (auxiliary drive belt)** – Must be the correct tension and damage free. A regular visual check is recommended.

● **Brakes** – If the brakes feel spongy or unusual in any way

get them checked rather than risk driving.

● **Engine oil** – Make sure you use the correct specification of engine oil (refer to the manufacturer's handbook).

● **Number plates** – Make sure your number plates are clean and undamaged.

● **Windows** – Check there are no cracks or chips in the windscreen within the driver's field of view (very small chips are acceptable).

● **Mirrors** – Make sure your rear view mirror is fixed securely and all mirrors can be adjusted.

Running costs such as fuel, repairs and servicing are very much influenced by how hard you use your car. The most important single factor is maintenance. There is no long-term saving in skimping on proper and adequate servicing: money-saving motoring doesn't mean cut-price motoring. A car must be in as near perfect condition as possible if it is to give its best performance and fuel consumption as well as maintain its value.

LOOKING AFTER YOUR CAR

19

Breakdown Prevention

THE TOP TEN CAUSES OF BREAKDOWN

Most common breakdown problems can be avoided with some simple pre-journey checks and regular maintenance. See page 130 for a list of regular checks you can make yourself to help you enjoy safer, worry-free motoring and minimise the risk of an inconvenient breakdown. However other, more complex problems may be require a visit to a garage. The following most common causes of breakdown suggest how you might be able to prevent a serious problem with your vehicle.

1. FLAT OR FAULTY BATTERY

Car batteries typically have a life of four to five years, so aim to replace the battery before it fails. Problems can arise from constant short journeys particularly in the winter. Making a regular long journey will help prolong battery life.

2. FLAT/DAMAGED TYRES

Check tread wear and adjust tyre pressure at least fortnightly, when the tyres are cold. Don't forget to check the spare, too. See Wheels and tyres on page 130 for further information.

3. KEY AND IMMOBILISER

Losing keys or locking them in the car can be extremely costly and inconvenient, too. Keep a spare set of keys in a safe place (not in the car), with a note of the key's identity number.

4. STARTING PROBLEMS

This problem is less common on modern cars but they can be vulnerable to over-fuelling if stopped shortly after starting. If the engine turns over normally, but doesn't start, and you know there is fuel available, try waiting 15 minutes to allow the excess fuel to evaporate.

5. STARTER MOTOR

Starter motors are usually robust, though they can fail through wear or bad connections. If you notice erratic starter operation, have it checked out by a garage.

6. FUEL

The most common problem here is drivers simply running out. Why not fill up when the gauge reaches half-empty, rather than waiting for the warning light? Misfuelling, usually by putting petrol into a diesel car, is common and can cause a lot of damage. It's important not to try starting the engine as you could cause even more damage.

7. ALTERNATOR/GENERATOR FAULTS

Persistent battery problems can indicate alternator/generator faults, as can dim headlights or slow wipers when the engine is idling. Always consult an expert.

8. COOLING SYSTEM

Faults such as perished hoses, radiator damage or faults with the fan should be picked up with regular checks.

9. CLUTCH

A clutch should last around 100,000 miles under normal driving conditions. However, failures can occur earlier, so any difficulties in changing gear should be investigated by a garage.

10. CAMBELT

The cambelt can require replacement at intervals as low as 40,000 miles, while failure of the belt could cause serious and very expensive engine damage.

LOOKING AFTER YOUR CAR

19

All-weather Driving

Motoring in all kinds of weather is a skill that comes with experience. Knowing how to cope when the weather suddenly changes is vital for safety. Keeping your car in good working order may prevent accidents and save vital repair costs.

SNOW AND ICE

The first fall of snow is always dangerous because the roads might not have been gritted. Even after gritting, they can still be very hazardous. Here's how to cope.

- **De-ice** – Never use boiling water to de-ice, it's dangerous and potentially damaging. Use a de-icer and a scraper.

- **Defrost properly** – Never start driving before your car is completely defrosted.

- **A clear view** – Check lights and number plates are clear.

- **Drive slowly** – It can take ten times longer to stop in icy conditions than on a dry road. Drive slowly, allowing extra room to slow down and stop.

- **Wheel spin** – Use highest gear possible to avoid wheel spin.

- **Manoeuvre gently** – Avoid harsh braking and acceleration in snow and ice.

- **Avoid wheel locking** – To brake on ice or snow without locking your wheels, get into a low gear earlier than normal, allow your speed to fall and use the brake pedal gently. If you skid, ease off the accelerator but do not brake suddenly.

FOG

Not only is your vision affected in fog, but other road users will have trouble seeing your vehicle. Fog can go from a light mist to a blanket very quickly.

- **Drive slowly** – If you must drive, drive slowly.

- **Visibility** – If this is very bad use rear fog lights as well as your dipped headlights. Avoid using full beam headlights as these reflect off the fog and reduce visibility further. Once

visibility improves, switch your
fog lights off to avoid dazzling
other people.

- **Turn on** – Wipers and
demisters.

RAIN

Brakes and tyres are much less
effective in the wet, so be aware.

- **Stopping distances** – These can
be doubled in rain as tyres have
less grip.

- **Slow down** – Slow gradually
to avoid skidding.

- **Headlights** – Switch them on
if visibility is reduced.

- **Oil slicks** – Rain is particularly
dangerous after a dry spell
when it loosens oil and debris
on the road to form oil slicks.

- **Don't prop the bonnet open
for too long in the rain** – the
engine will be more difficult
to start again if the electrics
become wet.

FLOODS

When conditions are bad enough
to create floods, please be aware
of the following:

- **Depth** –Don't drive into water
if you don't know its depth.

- **Drive slowly** – Stay in first gear
but keep the engine speed high
by slipping the clutch, this will
stop you from stalling.

- **Test your brakes** – When you
are through the flood, but
before you drive at normal
speed, always remember to
try your brakes.

HOT WEATHER

If the weather turns hotter:

- **Avoid drowsiness** – Keep
your vehicle well ventilated.

- **Soft surface** – Be aware that
the road surface may become
soft. If it rains after a dry spell
it may become slippery. These
conditions could affect your
steering and braking. Stay alert.

- **Overheating** – If the
temperature gauge is in the
red, find a safe place to stop
as soon as possible and switch
off the engine.

- **Transfer heat** – Keeping the car
heater and fan on high will help
transfer engine heat.

LOOKING AFTER YOUR CAR

19

Keeping Your Car Secure

KEEP IT SECURE AND SAVE MONEY

There are still more than two million vehicle-related thefts every year. The following advice will help you reduce the risk of becoming a victim of car crime. Making sure your vehicle is secure and parked in a safe place will help your insurance premiums and save you money.

CAR SECURITY HELPS

Theft rates are higher among cars that don't have effective security devices. The British Crime survey has shown that while 75% of main household cars had some kind of immobiliser fitted, only a third (32%) of cars that were stolen had immobilisers.

- **Before 1996** – Cars made before 1996 are at high risk of theft.

- **After 1996** – Cars made after 1996 are low theft risk. Those made after 1999 are a very low risk.

While most car crime is on the decrease, some specialist types of vehicle crime are bucking the trend. Both satellite navigation equipment theft and number plate theft are significant and growing problems.

- **Sat nav theft** – If you use portable satellite navigation equipment it's vital to take it with you whenever you leave the car. You must remove the cradle and suction pads, too, and clean any marks left on the windscreen or dashboard as thieves are known to look for these tell-tale signs and break in anyway.

- **Number plates** – If your plates are stolen contact the police immediately. It may seem a trivial matter at the time, but if the plates are used to change the identity of another vehicle you can expect to start receiving fixed penalty notices for parking, speeding etc. You may even be suspected of committing crimes yourself.

- **Catalytic converter theft** – The price of fuel may be falling now, but in these hard times the demand for precious metals, and parts that contain them, is rising – catalytic converters are new targets.

REDUCING THE RISK OF CRIME

Most crime is opportunist and is preventable with a little common sense and some basic precautions. Increasing your security will help your insurance premiums.

- **Lock-up and close-up** – Every time you leave the car, close the windows and lock the doors, even when stopping for only a short time such as at petrol stations.

- **Car keys are precious** – Remove them whenever you get out of the car and don't leave them on display at home.

- **Park somewhere safe** – Use a garage, a well-lit, busy street or a car park displaying the 'Park Mark' logo of the Safer Parking Scheme from the Association of Chief Police Officers (ACPO).

- **Use your alarm and immobiliser** – Use a mechanical immobiliser on its own if you have a low-risk vehicle or use it in conjunction with another form of security such as an alarm. Most mechanical immobilisers fit across the steering wheel. Remember to fit the device every time you leave the car. New cars are generally fitted as standard with effective immobilisers. If you have an older car, consider fitting a security system or upgrading one already fitted.

- **Obvious targets** – Remove mobile phones and sat navs from view.

- **Tempt no-one** – Loose change, music tapes or CDs attract thieves and the cost of repairs may be more than the value of the items taken.

LOOKING AFTER YOUR CAR

19

Getting the Most Out of Your Fuel

Whatever car you have there are a number of simple things you can do to reduce fuel consumption, CO_2 emissions and pollution.

DRIVE SMART

Once you've bought your car, there's a lot you can do to keep the cost of your fuel down:

- **Service your car regularly** – This will help maintain engine efficiency and cut fuel consumption.

- **Don't labour the engine** – Drive smoothly and change gear as soon as possible without labouring the engine – typically between 2000 and 2500rpm.

- **Load carefully** – Pack your roof rack carefully and remove a roof box when you don't need it.

- **Check tyre pressures regularly** – You can also adjust them to suit the load, as advised in your car's handbook.

- **Stick to 70mph on the motorway** – Keep within the law. By travelling at 80–85mph, fuel costs can increase by 25% or more.

- **Fill up before getting on the motorway** – You'll avoid higher pump prices.

There are four factors that affect how much you spend on fuel: price, type of fuel, the car's fuel consumption and the way you drive. Pump prices vary a lot around the country.

PETROL VS DIESEL

Diesel cars generally give you more miles to the gallon than petrol cars, though petrol cars are catching up.

- **Purchase Price** – New diesels may cost more than new petrol cars to buy but you should be able to sell them for more, too.

- **Servicing** – Diesel and petrol cars cost about the same to service, but a diesel car may need an oil change more often.

LOOKING AFTER YOUR CAR

19

- **Road tax** – Road tax is based on official CO_2 emissions and diesel cars generally produce less CO_2 because they are more efficient.

- **Company cars** – Diesel cars are popular with company car drivers. Despite the 3% surcharge due to their higher toxic emissions, diesel cars often cost less in company car tax overall because of their lower CO_2 emissions.

- **On the road** – Diesel engines warm up more quickly from a cold start than petrol which can take around a mile to get up to temperature. Once warm though, a petrol engine is cleaner than diesel, and gives out lower emissions. So, if you do frequent short journeys where the engine barely warms up, then a diesel could be better. If, however, you spend most of your time stuck in traffic around town, then a petrol car's best.

- **On the motorway** – fuel consumption is similar for petrol and diesel cars. Diesels are better for towing as they have more torque, while extreme performance is still petrol-driven territory.

LIQUEFIED PETROLEUM GAS

An alternative is LPG or Liquefied Petroleum Gas.

- **Cheaper fuel** – The gas is around half the price of petrol or diesel, but fuel economy will be around 25% less. Overall, LPG works out around a third cheaper – once you've done enough miles to recoup the extra cost of the car. The higher your annual mileage, the quicker you'll recover the extra outlay.

- **City driving** – LPG engines are comparable to the current generation of diesels and pre-Euro IV petrol engines, so good if you drive a lot in towns and cities, where low emissions are even more important.

- **Motoring abroad** – An LPG-fuelled car won't be allowed through the Eurotunnel, even if you can prove the tank has been disconnected or emptied. If you're travelling by ferry, check before you book.

LOOKING AFTER YOUR CAR

19

Choosing a Greener Car

Cars are one exception to the green rule that old is better than new. Modern cars are generally more fuel efficient and produce fewer emissions. A pre-1992 car with no catalytic converter can be 20 times more polluting than a new car.

FUEL EFFICIENCY

Look for a car with a fuel-efficient engine; it will be cheaper to run and a lot better for the environment.

- **Efficiency ratings** – Like fridges and washing machines, new cars now receive an efficiency rating ranging from A (for the most fuel-efficient models) to G (the most polluting). The information should be available at the showroom.

- **Vehicle Certification Agency** – The VCA has its own database of cars listing fuel efficiency, estimated fuel costs and environmental impact (see www.vcacarfueldata.org.uk for more information).

- **Society of Motor Manufacturers and Traders** – Its database has CO_2 emissions for all cars registered since 1997 which is useful if you are buying second-hand. However, in general, very old cars are significantly more polluting.

- **Automatic or manual?** – Automatic cars use about 10% more fuel than manuals, while cars with continuously variable transmission (CVT) use about 5% more. Consider an automatic transmission where the clutch and gear change occur without significantly increasing the fuel consumption of the car.

GREEN POWER

The best choice of eco-friendly fuel for you will depend on the sort of driving that you do.

- **Diesel** – Do not assume that diesel cars are necessarily the greener choice. Although they use less fuel than petrol cars, they produce more nitrogen oxides, particulates and other toxic emissions. Generally speaking, a diesel car is a better option if you do a lot of motorway driving. But if you live in an urban area, where air quality is more of a concern, go for petrol-driven cars.

- **Electric cars** – Worth considering if you only use a car for short trips. They can be charged from an ordinary socket, and costs work out around one pence a mile. Exemption from road tax, parking fees and congestion charges in some cities make them very cheap to run with one manufacturer claiming that you can recoup the cost of the car within a year.

- **Hybrid cars** – These combine an electric motor and battery with a petrol engine; the electric motor charges as you drive and then powers the car at lower speeds. They are pricier than standard cars to buy, but running costs are lower. Hybrids are ideal for town driving as the start/stop work uses the regenerative brakes

which recharge the batteries. If you do a lot of motorway driving, the benefits are less obvious.

WHICH WHEELS?

Buy the smallest car that suits your everyday needs. If you need a larger car once or twice a year, it may be cheaper to buy a smaller car and rent the larger one when you need it.

- **Four-wheel drives** – Burn between 4 and 14% more fuel than a standard vehicle with the same load-carrying capacity. As well as costing you more in fuel, they also incur higher vehicle excise duties and, in some areas, higher parking permit fees as well.

If you are buying a small family car, opting for a fuel-efficient model could shave almost 30% off your fuel bill. Greener cars not only save you money on fuel bills; they are also liable for less road tax.

LOOKING AFTER YOUR CAR

19

Responsible Driving

When it comes to reducing the environmental impact of your driving, it is not just what you drive that counts but also the way that you drive it. Follow these simple common sense tips to help cut your fuel bill.

CAR MAINTENANCE

The basic principle is this: the harder your engine has to work, the more fuel it has to burn, and the more CO_2 emissions are produced. So, if you go easy on your engine, you automatically use less fuel – saving you money and cutting the environmental cost of your driving.

A poorly maintained car is likely to use more fuel and pump out more pollution.

- **Regular checks** – See page 130 for a list of checks you can make yourself.

- **Regular servicing** – This will help keep your car in good working order.

- **Tyre pressure** – Soft tyres increase rolling resistance, making the engine use more fuel. See Wheels and tyres on page 130 for details.

- **Engine oil** – Using the recommended grade of engine oil can improve fuel efficiency by up to 2%.

BEFORE YOU GO

A little planning before you set off can help reduce fuel consumption.

- **Reduce load** – A heavy car uses more fuel, so don't carry anything you don't need. Clear the boot and take off bike racks or roof boxes when not in use.

- **Plan your route** – Getting lost makes you drive further and use more fuel. If you are going somewhere unfamiliar, take a few minutes to plan your journey before you leave. Visit theAA.com for a comprehensive route planner as well as up-to-date regional traffic news.

● **Avoid congestion** – If you can choose when to drive, steer clear of busy times. You'll use less fuel on a clear run than if you stop and start in traffic.

ON THE ROAD

Simple measures once you are on the road can also make a difference.

● **Don't dawdle** – Start your engine when you're ready to go and leave promptly. If you're likely to be stationary for more than three minutes, turn off the engine.

● **Think ahead** – Accelerate gently, and keep a close eye on the road ahead to avoid unnecessary braking. When you have to slow down or stop, release the accelerator in plenty of time, keeping your car in gear.

● **Avoid labouring the engine** – This makes it work harder, and burn more fuel, as well as putting extra strain on components such as the oil pump. Reducing revs can have a significant effect on fuel consumption. Try changing gear when the revs are around 2000rpm in a diesel car, or 2500rpm in a petrol car.

● **Slow down** – You use less petrol if you drive more slowly. When you are doing 70mph you could be using around 9% more fuel than at 60mph and 15% more than at 50mph.

● **Cut down on air con** – On calm roads, simply open the window. On the motorway, having the windows open increases drag so put on your air con for a few minutes, then switch to the blowers.

● **Turn off electrical gadgets** – Using the heated rear windows or headlights increases your fuel consumption.

According to the Department for Transport, following simple eco-driving tips could reduce the average driver's fuel costs by 8% – around £140 a year.

LOOKING AFTER YOUR CAR

19

Useful Contacts

- **AA Roadwatch** – Latest traffic and weather information. Call 84322 from mobile phones. Calls cost a minimum of 65p per minute. Mobile rates vary. (Lines open 24 hours a day, 365 days a year.) theAA.com

- **AA Membership enquiries** – 0870 5444 444. For enquiries by text phone 0800 328 2810.

- **DirectGov** – Includes information for motorists. Covers licensing, buying and selling vehicles, road safety, learners and new drivers, and more. www.direct.gov.uk

- **Driving Standards Agency (DSA)** – Driving tests for all vehicles. www.dsa.gov.uk

- **Driver Vehicle Licensing Agency (DVLA)** – Information on all vehicle and driving documentation, including driver licences and new vehicle registration. www.dvla.gov.uk

- **The Highways Agency** – Government agency responsible for operating and maintaining the strategic road network across England. www.highways.gov.uk

- **Safer Parking Scheme** – Lists approved Park Mark car parks across the UK. www.saferparking.com

- **Tyres-Online** – Technical information and tyre test reviews by brand. www.tyres-online.co.uk

- **Vehicle Certification Agency** – Testing and certification for vehicles. www.vca.gov.uk

- **Vehicle & Operator Services Agency (VOSA)** – For information and complaints regarding the MOT test and vehicle identity checks (VIC) and vehicle safety recalls. www.vosa.gov.uk